T0028510

25 Million Sparks evokes hope and inspiration from the most disquieting state of the human condition. Hanna's beautifully and masterfully interwoven narrative unveils the lives of three Syrian women surviving as refugees in the Za'atari camp in Jordan. Hanna's spotlight on their entrepreneurship chronicles the resilience of the human spirit against the inhumanity of war. As a two-time refugee, I am intimately familiar with the tragedy of conflict, the desperation of loss, and the curative effect of self-reinvention. *25 Million Sparks* is a testament to the power of hope and the power of women.

—Heather Ibrahim-Leathers
Founder of the Global Fund for Widows

—※—

Hanna tells the inspiring stories of three Syrian refugees, whose creativity and entrepreneurship show the strength of the human spirit to turn even the most difficult adversity into opportunity.

—Jonathan Levin
Dean of Stanford Graduate School of Business

—※—

Against the backdrop of the global refugee crisis, *25 Million Sparks* beautifully tells the moving story of three Syrian women working as entrepreneurs in a refugee camp in Jordan. The story of these remarkable women shines through the pages, with their devotion to building a better life for themselves and their families. And it calls us to action to address the disparate needs of more than 25 million refugees.

—John L. Hennessy
Former President of Stanford University

25 MILLION SPARKS

25 *Million Sparks* takes readers inside the Za'atari refugee camp to follow the stories of three courageous Syrian women entrepreneurs: Yasmina, a wedding shop and salon owner creating moments of celebration; Malak, a young artist infusing color and beauty throughout the camp; and Asma, a social entrepreneur leading a storytelling initiative to enrich children's lives. Anchored by these three inspiring stories, as well as accompanying artwork and poetry by Malak and Asma, the narrative expands beyond Za'atari to explore the broader refugee entrepreneurship phenomenon in more than twenty camps and cities across the globe. What emerges is a tale of power, determination, and dignity – of igniting the brightest sparks of joy, even when the rest of the world sees only the darkness.

A significant portion of the author's proceeds from this book is being contributed to support refugee entrepreneurs in Za'atari and around the world.

ANDREW LEON HANNA is a first-generation Egyptian American lawyer, entrepreneur, and author from Jacksonville, Florida. He is cofounder and CEO of DreamxAmerica, a Knight-Hennessy Scholar and Siebel Scholar at Stanford Graduate School of Business, and winner of the *Financial Times* and McKinsey Bracken Bower Prize. Hanna has been named to the *Forbes* 30 Under 30 list and graduated with honors from Harvard Law School, where he was an editor of the *Harvard Law Review*.

25 Million Sparks

Sparks

The Untold Story of Refugee Entrepreneurs

ANDREW LEON HANNA

Art by Malak
Poetry by Asma

CAMBRIDGE
UNIVERSITY PRESS

CAMBRIDGE
UNIVERSITY PRESS

University Printing House, Cambridge CB2 8BS, United Kingdom

One Liberty Plaza, 20th Floor, New York, NY 10006, USA

477 Williamstown Road, Port Melbourne, VIC 3207, Australia

314–321, 3rd Floor, Plot 3, Splendor Forum, Jasola District Centre, New Delhi – 110025, India

103 Penang Road, #05–06/07, Visioncrest Commercial, Singapore 238467

Cambridge University Press is part of the University of Cambridge.

It furthers the University's mission by disseminating knowledge in the pursuit of education, learning, and research at the highest international levels of excellence.

www.cambridge.org
Information on this title: www.cambridge.org/9781009181495
DOI: 10.1017/9781009181518

First published 2022

Printed in the United Kingdom by TJ Books Limited, Padstow Cornwall

A catalogue record for this publication is available from the British Library.

ISBN 978-1-009-18149-5 Hardback

For my mother and father,
who showed me the meaning of dignity.

CONTENTS

ix

Part IV Hope

The stories of Asma, Malak, and Yasmina – the three featured entrepreneurs in the Za'atari refugee camp in Jordan –
are based on oral histories as told by the trio in my interviews with them. (Pseudonyms or only first names have
been used in these and other entrepreneurs' stories for
privacy.) Most of the scenes in Za'atari and Syria are recon-
structed based on these interviews – all of which were
conducted in Arabic in the camp, audio recorded, and
archived – while some of the present-day scenes were
observed directly in the camp. I prefer this interview-centric
methodology because I believe it allows the entrepreneurs'
stories to be told with a primary emphasis on their own
powerful voices and perspectives.

Additionally, in this spirit of amplifying the entrepreneurs' perspectives, their creative work – Malak's art and
Asma's poetry – is featured throughout this book.

Finally, to further connect this book to the movement toward greater socioeconomic opportunity for refugee
communities, a significant portion of author proceeds is
being contributed to support refugee entrepreneurs in the
Za'atari camp and around the world.

CHAPTER 1

Angels of Za'atari

S trings of white lights, strewn from trailer top to trailer top, glimmer against the violet night sky. A classic Syrian tune, with its piercing accordion, strikes into the dry desert air. The sand shifts to the quickening beat of the darbuka.

It can mean only one thing: it's wedding season in Za'atari.

A cheering crowd gathers in a semicircle around the bride and groom, seated together in clear plastic chairs at the heart of the excitement. The bride wears a sparkling gold dress and a matching headscarf that shine in the darkness. Powder blue liner surrounds her beaming eyes, cast upward into the drama of the night. Camera flashes and compliments abound for the twenty-something young woman; her dress is gorgeous, makeup is flawless, hair is stunning, she is told. But the mastermind behind the look is nowhere to be found.

She is back, back in Saudi Market. Past the new falafel shop and toward the pink trailer with the emerald green dress hanging by the window. The accordions are only a faint echo now. Back beyond the trailer's wooden sign with its name painted on it – صالون الأنوار, "Salon of Lights" – and inside the purple door. Through the narrow zig-zag lane between the rainbow of puffy-bottomed dresses dangling from the ceiling. Back still, through the half-parted burgundy velvet curtain and into the beauty salon is where we finally find her . . . seated with her back resting against the glittery pink wall, she drinks her "shay" – her tea – peacefully.

She is Yasmina. Dressed in all black, with a black-and-gray striped hijab wrapped elegantly around her head, sitting like a queen in her castle. Silent power and confidence.

For most of her four decades on earth, Yasmina's life mission has been to prepare brides for their weddings. "Ever since I was a young girl in Syria, I loved dressing up my dolls and doing their hair. When I was fourteen, I told my parents I would one day open a salon. And I did." But she knows her place on wedding day; she likes to give her clients space.

Rather than attend the festivities, she spends this evening with her family in the salon. Her son Ashraf – thin with big energetic eyes and tightly wound curls, wearing a red-and-white Arsenal jersey – jumps onto one of the two perched brown leather seats in front of the long mirror, as if to make an announcement. He talks about his first day at soccer camp and how he scored his first goal. All to build up to his final line, one he does not hesitate to deliver: "Wallahee ana ahsan min Lionel Messi." "As God is my witness, I am better than Lionel Messi." Yasmina's husband Abdel, who is sitting next to her, nearly chokes on his tea in laughter.

Yasmina smiles – a sort of wise, bemused, even-tempered smile, as if to remind you not to get too high or too low in life. A smile of gratitude that recalls how she fled southern Syria while pregnant with Ashraf, how he was born prematurely at only seven months, and how she traveled to Za'atari with him in her arms. A smile of experience that tells her customers to trust her for their big days. "Believe me, sometimes a smile is enough."

She stands to get ready to head home, and glances at the clock on the wall. Back in District 5, the wedding is probably ending and her client should soon be heading home from the celebration. A celebration in a refugee camp. A celebration many outside the camp might find surprising, given the sufferings of war that led to the camp's very existence.

Yasmina laughs dismissively at the notion: "Syrians always find an excuse to celebrate." Then her face turns more serious, as if reflecting on her life's journey in just that moment:

"Fee wact lil huzn, wa fee wact lil farah."

"There is a time for sadness, and there is a time for happiness."

❊——❊——❊

Malak's studio is drenched in color.

An oval palette with dried paints of bright green, dull yellow, and burnt orange lays on the chair. Half-squeezed tubes of paints called *French ultramarine blue* and *flamingo pink* and *alizarin crimson* are piled by the foot. Works of art are scattered on the floor underneath the easel with her blank white canvas: a pencil drawing of a United Nations (UN) aid worker in his light blue vest, a black-and-white charcoal drawing of a man with a half-shaven beard, a painting of a woman with a thorny red rose pressed against her closed eyelid.

This studio in Za'atari District 11 doubles as a shared bedroom with Hoda, one of Malak's eleven older sisters. Hoda frequently comes home to an obstacle course of paint brushes, drawings, and assorted frames – which had been an ongoing source of sibling argument, until she simply got used to the treacherous path to bed. Malak is the youngest daughter, so "I'm in a good spot – all the attention is on me," she says with a guilty laugh illuminating her round face. Besides, Hoda is too proud of her little sister's art to stay upset.

The studio's business model starts with Malak painting what is in her heart. Many times that leads to a flurry of orders from customers around the world through her Instagram and Facebook pages – a process coordinated by the studio's manager: Malak's neighbor, best friend, and biggest fan, Roaa. Often it leads to a sale at an auction or exhibition, some of which are hosted in Za'atari and others in Amman, the capital city of Jordan.

But usually, as in the case of Malak's current project, revenue is a distant afterthought. This project will be presented in just an hour at a community forum for girls about the harms of child marriage, a practice that leaves girls open to abuse, threatens their mental and physical health, and interrupts their education. Wearing a turquoise headscarf and navy dress, Malak sits on the ground and uses a midnight blue colored pencil to put the finishing touches on the last of twenty comic-style drawings. This one is a young girl in a teal wedding dress looking sadly, longingly up at a magnificent full moon by the ocean. "People often don't like you to advise them directly, but you can get to them through art." At least she hopes so, because the girls of Za'atari have talents waiting to be discovered. "When you find the gift God gave you, you can do amazing things."

"Time to go sister!" Hoda enters the doorway with a knock. Five feet of constant energy, Malak hurriedly puts her pencil down, gathers her drawings, and stumbles to the door. "Trust me, I'll clean up later." Malak's piercing eyes smile knowingly at Hoda. An eager smile. Eager to awaken the spirit within Za'atari, one drop of color at a time. Certainly too eager to clean her trailer.

If you would have told a younger Malak that this is what her life would look like at age twenty-three, that bright light in her eyes might have flickered. Her studio now is very different from the lush garden where she would paint back at home in Damascus. Za'atari is not where she wanted to be, not by a long shot. "I kissed the ground of my house in Syria before I left. I cried so much into the wind outside the house that my sisters thought it was raining. I would have rather died than go to Za'atari."

"But I always had the paper and crayons that I brought with me from Syria." With those in hand, her dreams would evolve and take hold. Now at once a businesswoman, an artist, a community leader, a university student, a medical professional in training, and, yes, a refugee, Malak – which means "angel" in Arabic – is not just living in Za'atari. She is enlivening it.

⚹ — ✳ — ⚹

Sitting alone in the center of her trailer, on a chocolate-colored cushion resting atop the chocolate-colored carpet, Asma looks down at a children's book. Her soft brown eyes dart across page after page in sheer concentration. It was a quick rehearsal for the performance to come. A rare moment of silence in Trailer 6.4, District 8, Za'atari.

Suddenly, without a word from Asma, the trailer around her is transformed. Children's laughter and stomping against the dirt outside grows louder and louder until the trailer walls shake slightly. The wooden door creaks open. Five young boys take off their shoes and dive into the open space in front of Asma, as is their weekly ritual. Her living room had become a magical escape for them.

"Ahlan wa sahlan, ya Sammy." "Welcome, Sammy." Asma greets each of them, her face having instantaneously switched from focus to a smile. If Yasmina's smile is wise, and Malak's is eager, Asma's is soft and infectiously joyful. More and more children pour in, and last through the door are two of Asma's favorite students: her eldest daughters, Tamara and Maya. Tamara is shorter, older, and gentler, while Maya is taller, younger, and more playfully mischievous. Returning from taekwondo practice, they are wearing matching white uniforms with yellow belts. They quickly say their hellos and head to the back room, reemerging in matching ruby dresses with big ruby bows in their hair. They take turns giving Asma a hug before sitting cross-legged with their friends.

It's time to begin. "Yalla, ya shabaab." "Come on, children." With three words, as if Asma possesses a supernatural gravitational pull, the children gather to sit in a more organized circle surrounding her. She grabs ahold of her baby boy, Mohammed, and puts him firmly in her lap as she reaches over him to turn to the first page. The magic begins.

"This story is about a conversation between a boy named Samir and his mom. It is called *A Plane That Brings Love*."

Asma's voice rises and falls as she reads the story, with the passion of a once-in-a-lifetime audition. The children concentrate, spellbound by her performance, immersed in a world far removed from the Za'atari heat. At each page, Asma smoothly rotates the book toward the kids so they can enjoy the illustrations accompanying the dialogue:

> *"Mom, I want to drive an army airplane when I grow up,"* Samir says.
>
> يقول سمير: "يا أمي، أريد قيادة طائرة عسكرية عندما أكبر."

Tamara suddenly stands and scurries to the kitchen. She returns with a water jug and glasses for the group. Always a gracious host. Asma continues:

> *"But I will be a pilot of love, not war. I will draw red hearts and spread them everywhere from my plane. I will spread happiness, love, hope, and peace. So the little boys and girls can play in peace. So the birds flying around can sing in peace."*

"لكنني سأكون طيارًا للحب، وليس للحرب. سأوجه القلوب الحمراء وأنشرها في
كل مكان من طائرتي. سأنشر السعادة والحب والأمل والسلام. لذلك يمكن للفتيان
والفتيات الصغار اللعب في سلام. لذلك يمكن للطيور المحلقة الغناء في سلام."

Upon reaching the final page, she holds up the book to show
a cartoon illustration of a boy with brown aviator goggles
parachuting down onto the Syrian hills, as his mom waits for
him with open arms. His parachute is in the form of a red
heart with the word "love" – حب – labeled on it in three
places.

> *"Yes! I will be pilot of love, not war. So my country will be*
> *more beautiful. A country of hope, happiness, love, and*
> *peace."*[1]

"نعم فعلا! سأكون طيار الحب، وليس الحرب. لذلك سيكون بلدي أكثر جمالا. بلد
الأمل والسعادة والحب والسلام."

For a second or two, the words hang in the air. Asma closes
the book: "Al Nihaya." "The End."

In an instant, the spell is lifted. The kids graciously
thank Asma and begin to gather their things and leave,
playfully pushing one another on their way out. In the
moments after their departure, as their laughter fades in
the distance, Asma is alone again for just a few seconds.

She thinks back to when she was a girl two decades
ago in the town of Dara'a, and what her education meant to
her. How she would sleep in her school uniform because she
was so excited for the next day. How she dreamt one day she
would become a teacher, but worried she lacked the confidence. "I loved school. But in class when the teacher would
ask a question and I knew the answer, I would have to wait
until at least one person raised her hand first." Now she is

boldly reinventing herself as a social entrepreneur and poet, leading a storytelling initiative that is expanding throughout Za'atari. "I want every girl to complete her education. Everyone should fulfill her dream."

In that brief moment of quiet, Asma looks up and whispers a prayer of thanks for the chance to "tashaja," to "encourage" . . . to gently uplift children toward the dreams they might otherwise have forgotten.

⁂

Welcome to Za'atari. مرحبا بكم في الزعتري

Here, in the desert heat, a community was born in the swell of crisis. Situated in Jordan just seven and a half miles south of the Syrian border, the camp – a two-square-mile rectangle divided into twelve districts – is nestled in the very heart of the Middle East.[2] A twenty-first-century refuge where ancient empires once reigned.

A consequence of the Syrian civil war, Za'atari began in summer 2012 as a barren place devoid of activity and, more fundamentally, lacking in hope. It is a place originally meant to exist only temporarily, but one that has nonetheless persisted till today as the Syrian war cruelly trudges forward into its second decade. Over the years – though extraordinary challenges persist in the camp – Za'atari residents would transform the settlement into a hotbed of entrepreneurship. Thousands of startups and social initiatives now line the streets in trailers, which are the ubiquitous corrugated aluminum mobile housing units also referred to as "caravans." This entrepreneurial movement is the story told in this book. Yasmina, Malak, and Asma are parts of that movement, innovating to infuse celebration, art, and education into their improbable desert home. And they, too, are parts of a much broader story of refugee entrepreneurs activating camps and cities around the world, from Middle Eastern towns to the American Rust Belt and everywhere in between.

These three women's work has helped uplift the Za'atari community, but that outcome was far from inevitable. The start of their stories was the start of every refugee's story: pain. Like any striving entrepreneur knows, pain is not just pain – it is an opportunity. But before they could tap into the powerful sparks within them, their periods of utter darkness were all too real. Refugees endure some of the harshest periods of darkness a human being can experience in this life.

Darkness is where this story begins.

Part I

Darkness

*No one leaves home unless
home is the mouth of a shark.*
—Warsan Shire, "Home"

CHAPTER 2

Olive Trees

D ara'a – درعا – was a fine place to dream.

Right at the southwestern edge of Syria near the Jordanian border, Dara'a was just connected – and just secluded – enough. It was a traveler's midpoint between Syria's capital city of Damascus and Jordan's capital city of Amman. An at-times buzzing crossroads for business and cultural exchange between neighboring nations.

But Dara'a bore little resemblance to the two major Middle Eastern cities it sat between. It was a relatively quiet town of about 75,000,[1] mostly unknown on the world's stage. A place with its share of challenges, to be sure – recent periods of drought not the least among them.[2] But a place with a community and a spirit about it, where often people knew one another growing up. A place built on agriculture, where gardens growing countless fruits and vegetables were passed down among families from generation to generation.

A place where one could escape the summer heat in the cool shade of the olive trees.

That was what a young Asma would do, at least. For her, life in Dara'a was simple. Her dad was a respected teacher and she lived in an affluent neighborhood, with relatives all around her. Her house contained a spacious garden, where there stood the brightest symbol of her memories of Syria: an olive tree. "We used to climb it and pick olives together. It was so much fun."

It was amidst that period of comfort that she found her first loves: books and school. Every morning, she would walk to the schoolhouse with her sisters, and every evening she would walk back with a new stack of books under her arm. At home, aside from playing in the garden and eating supper, she would sit alone, reading everything she could get her hands on. Only when she became exhausted from reading would she turn out the lights and fall sleep. She was so enamored with school and everything about it that she would sleep in her school uniform; she simply could not wait to start the next day.

Only one problem. An all too familiar problem for children who aren't blessed – or perhaps cursed – with inordinate confidence: she had trouble speaking up in class. "I was not brave. I was shy." Still, a dream formed within her: that she would grow in confidence and become a teacher like the ones she was so sorely afraid to address in the classroom. A teacher like her dad was.

As the years passed, though, her education stalled, and her dream was laid to the side. "That got interrupted. I got married when I was fifteen years old, so I stopped going to school." In the ensuing years, Asma did not let her circumstances keep her from breathing some life into her passion for reading and writing. "I finished my education at home. I always had books with me, and I would always write notes in my journals." Meanwhile, she was adjusting to family life the best she could. She would turn her focus toward becoming the ultimate teacher for her daughter, Tamara, as her husband was gone at work. She would spend her days reading to Tamara, channeling her love of education into her young child.

Asma does not stop to think much about her time in Dara'a; because of the way that time would end, she avoids the topic. "I like to forget," she says with a kind smile hiding her grief. But when she does think of the good times back at home, she remembers just how sweet they could be. Picking olives in the garden as a child, without a care.

Nearby, and several years older than Asma, was Yasmina. Yasmina had time to establish even deeper roots in Syria before leaving. In her early thirties when she departed, Yasmina had not only dreamed; she had lived out her dream.

She, too, discovered her calling at an early age. Yasmina's obsession with styling her dolls as a girl led her straight to launching a salon and wedding dress shop as a young woman. Though she did not have as much experience as others when her business first opened, she was up for the challenge. "I learned quickly." Yasmina ran her venture with great success, planning weddings and preparing brides across Dara'a for their special days.

Each appointment brought another radiant woman anticipating her moment, trusting Yasmina like a sister. Yasmina herself would get married and have two children, Hamid and Laila, living a life of relative peace and prosperity.

The youngest of the trio, Malak learned to dream not in Dara'a, but just a bit further north in Damascus. Her memories of life in her hometown span a shorter duration, since she was only a teenager when she left. But she, too, is persuaded she found her life's mission early on.

Malak lived in a humming home with eleven older sisters and an older brother. Her house had a well next to it and a generator for electricity. Like Asma's house growing up, Malak's included a large garden. Malak, her siblings, and her mother and father grew a range of fruits and vegetables – including, yes, olives. "Our life in Syria was a routine life: school, home, garden. It was a good life."

The school part was a mixed bag for Malak. Math class: not her style. Geography class: also not her style, except the days when her teacher would ask the class to draw maps on large pieces of construction paper. Malak loved that, and everyone else loved watching her. She started to realize that perhaps God had given her a specific talent and joy that should drive her life.

Art class, then: definitely her style. Malak shined, and her art teacher noticed. This teacher and others would invite her to place her creations all around the school – much to the appreciation of her classmates, the faculty, and the staff. "They were always asking me to decorate the classes and the hallways." It was then that Malak developed her dream: to create her own art studio in Damascus. As far as everyone around her could tell, she was well on her way.

Then, in a rush, night fell upon Syria. Change came swiftly and it came painfully. It came in the month of March, the year 2011. And it was triggered by, of all things, the acts of fifteen schoolchildren in, of all places, the calm town of Dara'a.

But to understand that change, one must venture back three more months and a couple thousand miles, across the Mediterranean Sea to the small North African nation of Tunisia. There, on a hot day in December 2010, a twenty-six-year-old man named Mohamed Bouazizi was at work.

A street vendor in a quiet Tunisian town, Mohamed was, as is reported, accused by city inspectors of not paying a fine.[3] Believing this to be a clear request for a bribe, Mohamed refused to pay.[4] In response, the inspectors seized his electronic scale and crates of fruit.[5] A crowd gathered, and the confrontation led to a policewoman allegedly slapping him on the face and insulting his father, who had died when Mohamed was three years old.[6] Mohamed went to the provincial government office to file a complaint.[7] But he was refused entry.[8] "Above all," as *Foreign Policy* summarized in an article on his life, Mohamed was "a repressed entrepreneur."[9] It was at that moment of despair – symbolically in front of the government building – that Mohamed decided he could no longer bear the repression.[10]

Mohamed lit himself on fire using paint thinner, and died as the flames engulfed him.[11]

That moment is looked back upon as the moment that ignited the Arab Spring, and the region would never be the same. The Middle East and North Africa was electrified with a passion for a voice in democratic government, an end to public corruption, better economic conditions, and greater civil liberties. In Tunisia it was called the Jasmine Revolution, and protests erupted until twenty-three-year president Zine al-Abidine Ben Ali stepped down and fled the country to make way for democratic elections.[12] Egypt was next. Tahrir Square in Cairo was packed with tens of thousands of protestors.[13] Less than three weeks later, after the death of 846 civilians and 26 policemen in clashes, Hosni Mubarak's rule of almost thirty years would come to an end.[14] Two of the longest-tenured leaders in the region were, all but overnight, out of power.

اجاك الدور يا دكتور.

It's your turn doctor.

Four words in red graffiti on the wall of a school in little Dara'a.[15] Words, along with other revolutionary slogans, directed toward Syria's president, Bashar al-Assad, a physician by training. Words painted as a peaceful protest by about fifteen teenage boys.[16]

Words that changed Syria forever.

Already on high alert given the winds of resistance blowing across the region, the Syrian government responded quickly and violently. Ben Ali's more than two decades of rule ended, Mubarak's nearly three decades of rule ended, but the Assad family's then four decades would not go down so swiftly.[17] The fifteen boys in Dara'a were arrested, jailed, and tortured.[18] In response, many in the town erupted in outrage, marching in protest of the children's detention.[19]

Just as Mohamed Bouazizi's fiery death signaled the start of the Jasmine Revolution, a singular moment in

Dara'a – not Damascus, not Aleppo, but humble Dara'a – would come to signal the start of the Syrian chapter of the Arab Spring. Suddenly, Dara'a had transformed from a quiet town to the "cradle of the revolution."[20] International media later called the events in Dara'a the "spark that lit the flame."[21] The town was labeled the "heartland of Syria's revolution."[22]

Tensions escalated over the coming weeks, as police violently cracked down on protesters and, in response, some opposition supporters started to take up arms.[23] The conflict became all too real for residents of Dara'a in late April. Army tanks drove into the town.[24] Troops cut water and electricity, as well as phone lines, and went door-to-door looking for protesters.[25] Snipers on mosques and in helicopters loomed overhead, according to Dara'a residents.[26] As one shared with *The New York Times*, "There are bodies in the streets we can't reach; anyone who walks outside is getting shot at."[27]

This ten-day siege left hundreds dead, and the bloodshed only escalated from there.[28] Violence between government forces and newly formed opposition groups in the region heightened to a point at which shellings and bombings were commonplace.[29] Over the next two years, it became clearer and clearer to many families in Dara'a, Damascus, and across the area that their primary hope of safety would be to leave.

This is the context in which the Za'atari refugee camp was born. Just across the Syrian border in Jordan, close enough to hear the sound of artillery from Dara'a at night, Za'atari was established in July 2012.[30] As fighting escalated, the population exploded later that year and in

2013 – with the camp growing from settlements in only what is today's northwest quadrant, to expanding into the southwest, to filling out the full rectangle.[31] The overwhelming number of Syrian families fleeing to Jordan led to the creation of a second refugee camp, called Azraq, nearby.[32]

As put in the poem "Home Was Your Refuge, Now They Call You Refugee" by British Indian poet Nikita Gill: "Home is where / You had to teach your children / How to run from men who are dressed / In war and blood."[33] This was the lived experience of the residents of Dara'a, Damascus, and Syria more broadly, and the transformation from calm to unrest to war happened before anyone could prepare for it.

Asma, Yasmina, and Malak prefer not to talk much about their sudden departure.

Asma was the first of the three to go. It was just twenty days after her second daughter Maya's birth, but there was no choice or time to prepare. Her house had been burned down, and she had lost most of her belongings – including her journals. Asma joined a group of family members and neighbors who were huddling together to make the dangerous trip to Za'atari. For baby Maya, who had just entered the world, this was the most offensive of beginnings: to be kicked out of your home, at no fault of your own. As Asma summarizes her family's move: "I hated the way I came here."

Yasmina held out a few months longer, continuing to operate her salon and wedding shop but carefully watching as the residents around her began to flee and the wedding celebrations dwindled.

She was pregnant with her third child, Ashraf, when she could hold out no longer. "When things turned to be very bad around Ramadan 2013, we left. I was seven months pregnant, my son had just had an operation, and my husband was sick." It could not have been a worse time to have her life completely uprooted.

Malak left Damascus around then, too. Her parents were worried for her and her siblings' future. "Things changed, and it became very hard to live in Syria. My mom was worried about us." She remembers the moment she left her luxurious home, unwilling to accept that the next morning she would wake up in a tent inside a refugee camp.

"The time I left Syria was really hard. I was crying. It was a very hard experience. Harder than hunger."

"But thank God I was able to forget."

⊱ —— ✳ —— ⊰

Dara'a and Damascus lived on beyond the departure of Asma, Yasmina, Malak, and others, but without so many of the people and activities that once brought life to those places. Without Yasmina's salon or Asma's passion for education or Malak's art.

Yasmina's house was destroyed. Asma's was burned to the ground. Malak's dad has a video of their family's former home on his cell phone, sent by a friend who stayed back. He shows it to those who visit their current home in Za'atari, with a mix of pride in what he had built and sorrow in what he has lost. A sort of reminder that, lest any visitor think this is normal to him, it is not; it is his worst nightmare, the type of nightmare that could happen suddenly to anyone living a "normal life." Yet, still, he holds a resilient pride in emerging on the other side and entertaining guests yet again, regardless of whether the center of gravity is a spacious home in Damascus or a trailer in Za'atari.

As the shaky camera image on his phone moves from one room to the next, the visuals are clear: rubble, busted walls, belongings strewn about and covered in ash. Nothing stands untarnished.

Nothing, perhaps, but the olive trees outside. A reminder of the people that had once breathed life into Syria – the girls like a young Asma who would climb their limbs and gather their fruits, and the emerging artists like Malak who would paint under their shade.

A symbol of peace and life still standing amidst a place destroyed, in the blink of an eye, by an unexpected war. Tunisian poet Asma Jelassi and Syrian poet Widad Nabi, who fled Aleppo during the war, wrote about the mix of haunting reminders and sweet memories that accompany distant thoughts of home. In their words:

> Dejection is
> To visit the ruins of your house in a dream
> And return without having its dust clung to your
> Hands.[34]

CHAPTER 3

Gray Walls

Yasmina was seven months pregnant when she closed the doors of her salon and wedding shop, not knowing if or when she might return. The journey to Za'atari was a difficult one for anyone. But the journey to Za'atari while pregnant was almost unbearable.

Uncertain about the future, Yasmina and her family left all that they knew behind. They hurriedly threw their most precious belongings into black trash bags. Her husband, despite being ill during that time, drove his pickup truck that he used for work to the front of the house and filled its bed with the bags.

They would drive from village to village, doing their best to avoid "checkpoints" – the often-violent physical impediments set up by armed groups that frequently demand money or goods in order to allow people to pass.[1] "We stayed with families who would welcome us in, or in abandoned schoolhouses." Yasmina, physically and emotionally exhausted by her pregnancy, increasingly felt a sense of guilt: "I did not want to make the family stay behind because of me."

Yasmina would give birth to Ashraf prematurely in a guesthouse in a nearby village. Alongside her family, she would make the final hour-long portion of the trek to Za'atari on foot while carrying Ashraf. Once on the access road, she saw in the distance what she had been waiting for: the drab gray concrete walls surrounding the Za'atari camp. Gray walls enclosing what would become her new life, a far cry from the home she left in Dara'a.

In Za'atari's early existence in particular, it was a barren place. It was a plot of desolate desert land dotted with stained-white tents labeled with the iconic light blue "UNHCR" logos, representing the UN refugee agency (the United Nations High Commissioner for Refugees) that partners with the Jordanian government to operate the camp. As the UNHCR's representative in Jordan acknowledged when the camp first opened:

> We are the first to admit that it is a hot desolate location. Nobody wants to put a family who has already suffered so much in a tent, in the desert, but we have no choice. We are prepared to provide the most basic of assistance and maximum protection, but we have to work with what we have.[2]

Like all camps, Za'atari was meant to be temporary: a refuge for Syrians for a short time until they were able to return to their home country. But no one knew when the Syrian war would end, and so life carried with it a shadow of uncertainty at all times.

Life in Za'atari was rigid. Mornings saw long lines for meager bread rations, and daily protests symbolized the community's low morale. Even the geography of the camp itself was regimented – divided evenly into clean rectangles. Exit and entry was generally forbidden.

At the northern end of Za'atari was the "base camp," where volunteers, wearing their orange and red and blue vests symbolizing their respective aid organizations, scrambled to put together plans for the day: erecting tents for those who needed shelter, distributing rations, and setting up provisional health care facilities.

Za'atari residents elected councils to represent them in discussing the camp's early challenges with Jordanian government and UN officials. But many grew restless in the face of inadequate provisions for their families. One sit-in of dozens of residents blocked the main access road to protest the limited food rations. As a young resident told a journalist, "We are being given three pieces of bread a day and told to fend for ourselves. How many nights can I put my son to bed with hunger [pangs]?"[3] Sometimes these demonstrations would become violent.[4] Rufut, a security guard who works for the Jordan branch of the nonprofit Save the Children, recounted the tensions early on: "It was difficult back then. There were [protests] almost every day."[5]

Beyond the challenges of food and shelter, there were other deep-seated issues in Za'atari – many of which persist, albeit to a lesser degree, today. Education access was one. With limited educational programming especially in the early months, over three-quarters of children in Za'atari were out of school, leaving their academic progress to diminish and their aspirations to stall.[6] Child labor became a major issue as families, especially large ones, were desperate for income and food security.[7] Child marriage – early marriage before the age of eighteen, which was already a challenge in Syria before the war – accelerated as families grew unable to provide for their children.[8] They sometimes saw these marital arrangements as a way to secure their daughters food, security, and "sponsorship" to leave the camp and live with a husband in Jordan.[9] This practice frequently leads to serious health risks, sexual violence, and exploitation, along with the deprivation of education and personal growth.[10] As one woman told Save the Children:

> I was married when I was fifteen years and had two [miscarriages] . . . . I was not able to think clear[ly] and did not know if it was my fault. I am nineteen now with a nine-month-old baby. [I] had a very hard delivery . . . . I still feel I am too young to be a mother.[11]

Health was another concern. Mental health challenges were and continue to be a major obstacle in Za'atari, where a notably high percentage of children between five and seventeen years old face issues with anxiety on a daily basis.[12] This level of anxiety – often leading to shorter attention spans and drifting focus in class, for example – is tied closely to experiences of trauma in being forced to flee home with grave safety concerns and minimal resources. Virtually everyone in Za'atari, too, has a story of intimate loss. The impermanence of living in the camp also contributes, as people experience a sort of "mental limbo" – living between modes of hoping for a return to Syria, to praying they will be resettled by the UNHCR to another country, to settling in for the long haul in Za'atari on the assumption they may never be able to leave.

Access to both mental and physical health care is limited, and was especially so in the early days when there were few health care facilities. Residents with disabilities, in particular, suffered greatly. Medical devices and services that are critical to the lives and well-being of individuals with disabilities are, and were, often scarce and/or ineffective. One report conducted a few years into the camp's existence indicated that about a quarter of Za'atari residents needed "physio, occupational and speech therapies," with many more needing mental health and psychosocial support and assistive devices.[13] Among this group, roughly a quarter were unable to access even one specialized service.[14] Consider Osama, who has several family members with disabilities: his sister has Down syndrome, his uncle cannot walk, and his aunt cannot speak.[15] Osama's family, at the time of his interview with a journalist shortly after arriving in Za'atari, had not been able to procure a wheelchair for his uncle.[16] As Osama explained, "[M]y uncle – he needs other things. He can only sit. He cannot use the bathroom."[17] Without much in the way of health care support, Osama, a young man himself, and his elderly grandmother were left to take care of the family the best they could in their trailer ... mostly on their own.

Or consider Salma. In her first few months at the camp, Salma would mostly lie on her back in her makeshift bed, with sheets covering her legs, and look longingly at the outside world through the slight opening in her tent. She was paralyzed from the neck down from injuries sustained due to a bombing back home in Dara'a. In a temporary shelter in Za'atari at the time of her interview, her children and husband cared for her, encouraging her and doing whatever therapy they could with her. Salma could not help but feel a sense of sadness about her inability to do the physical things she used to do, as she explained to a reporter: "I do not go outside much. It is difficult for me to see other parents carrying their children . . . . I am here, useless." Still, she remained a brave and resilient woman, and a caring mother. And her husband and children were always there by her side; with their love surrounding her, there was hope. As she shared an old photograph of her and her husband arm in arm, her face lit up with a graceful glow: "Ana bi hibhu kateer, wallahee." "I love him very much, truly."[18]

Finally, job opportunities were scarce as well. The few formally available jobs were those related to the administration of the camp.[19] Za'atari residents had arrived at an entirely new community – one with no economy, no businesses, and no road map for how to earn a living for one's family.

When adding all these factors together, Za'atari made for a particularly distressing experience early in the camp's existence. Just days, weeks, months before they arrived, many residents of Za'atari were living comfortably in Syria; now they were struggling to survive in a makeshift community run by strangers. Their movement, work, food –

all dictated by people they had never met, all because of a war they could not control.

——*

"Thank God, he survived." Back in the quiet of her tent, Yasmina prayed with gratitude for the fact that Ashraf lived through the terrible journey. He was healthy.

But it did not make the first few weeks and months much easier. She remembers vividly her first days in Za'atari: "When I came here, it was a very challenging time. I wanted to go home, daytime or nighttime. To go back." She worried the environment surrounding Hamid, Laila, and Ashraf would stifle their growth, from the lack of educational opportunities to the camp's scorching, sandy conditions. "I couldn't even breathe."

No longer did she have the day-to-day joys of the salon and wedding shop. But she was confident that one day soon, she would return. She continued to hold off on beginning to try to find work, praying she would soon head home to a peaceful Syria.

Asma, meanwhile, dealt with the worst moment of her life in her early days in Za'atari. Shortly after arriving, she left the camp with her family to try to settle in nearby Jordanian host communities. But the lack of opportunity there was prohibitive. She was pregnant when she returned to Za'atari, and she soon began feeling ill. She tried to get treatment at a nearby local hospital, but by the time she was able to be seen it was too late. "When I came here, I was so depressed. I lost my child. It worsened my depression."

She feared the worst for her daughters Tamara and Maya, believing all hope for their education had died . . . and worrying about what might happen if either of them were to become ill at the camp.

And Malak – Malak simply could not come to grips with how her life had transformed. "Every morning I would wake up and see the white of the tent, instead of the ceiling of my house, and I wouldn't know where I was." Malak would have nothing to do for hours and days and weeks on end. Without any schooling options and separated from her friends, Malak would sit alone in a small corner of the tent . . . and draw, releasing her emotions through her art from morning until night.

"When we came here, to live in the tent, I didn't go to school. So I was always at home."

Art was her refuge from the anxiety of it all. She would learn by watching YouTube videos on her smartphone – mimicking the artists she saw. Anything to pass the time. Anything to attempt to express the mixture of emotions inside her.

"All I could do was my art."

CHAPTER 4

Global Crisis

A three-year-old boy in a red T-shirt and blue shorts on a sunny day at the beach, laying lifeless face down on the sand. His face in the water, his legs on the sand. Washed up on the shore. A single picture that tormented hearts around the world. A harrowing symbol of the refugee crisis that could not be ignored.

The boy was a Syrian of Kurdish ethnicity named Aylan. When the Syrian war began, his family moved to Kobani, a city on the border between Syria and Turkey. Because of fighting there between the brutal Islamic State of Iraq and Syria (ISIS) and Kurdish groups, he and his family packed into an inflatable boat to flee for Greece.[1] The boat capsized about five minutes into the journey.[2] Aylan, along with his mother and brother, drowned in the Mediterranean Sea, survived by only his father Abdullah – who was unable to save them.[3]

Aylan's last photo was all over television screens and app notifications in September 2015. It was a photo that "woke up the world to the Syrian refugee crisis."[4] Donations to humanitarian organizations skyrocketed briefly. Then-prime minister David Cameron of Britain and then-president François Hollande of France spoke out about the world's responsibility to Aylan and so many like him.[5]

Three years later in 2018, in America, a new set of troubling images captured the world's attention. Children behind bars in overcrowded detention centers, with no parents in sight. Again, people from across the political spectrum were appalled. Conservatives and liberals alike criticized President Donald Trump's "zero-tolerance policy" – in which parents merely accused of crossing the border illegally were punished by being separated from their children – as "cruel" and "immoral."[6] President Trump backtracked, aiming to pin the blame for family separation and detention conditions on the preceding administration.[7] Bipartisan outrage continued and there was a strong desire for rectification; no one believed kids should be treated in such a way.[8]

The images helped to explain what the appalling statistics could not: we are living in a refugee crisis – the greatest global refugee crisis in the history of the world.[9]

Today, more people than at any other time in world history have been forcibly displaced from their homes. These estimated 82.4 million individuals have been forced to flee their communities because of war, violence, conflict, or persecution.[10] For them, leaving home was not a choice; it was a fight for survival that anyone in their shoes would have had to endure. The UNHCR has noted that today more than "one percent of humanity" (one in ninety-seven people) is forcibly displaced,[11] the highest fraction of the world's population to be displaced since the agency started keeping tabs on these numbers over five decades ago.[12]

Among this broader category of displaced people are a group – included within it all of the residents of Za'atari – who have been forced not just to leave their home communities but to cross the borders of their home countries: "refugees." Yasmina, Malak, and Asma represent just 3 of nearly 80,000 stories of darkness across Za'atari.[13] And these Za'atari stories are merely 80,000 of the now-well-over 25 million refugee stories across the globe.[14] Over half of refugees are children.[15] Many live in refugee camps – settlements that temporarily house refugees. The majority provisionally stay in urban settings in "host" nations, where they are allowed to live until they can return home.[16] Very few are permanently resettled to new countries by the UNHCR. More than four million additional individuals – like the Central American families in detention centers in the US – are "asylum seekers," meaning they have come to another country for protection but their statuses as refugees have not yet been legally determined.[17]

The causes of this refugee crisis are truly global; it takes a worldwide analysis to tell the story. Troublingly, the crisis is worsening. An average of more than 30,000 people were displaced every day in 2020.[18] The number of refugees has risen from 25 million to 26.4 million just over the course of the writing of this book, as its title attests. Considering a slightly longer time horizon, the number of displaced people in the world has more than doubled in just the last decade or so.[19] Crises in Myanmar, Yemen, Venezuela, Afghanistan, Somalia, the Democratic Republic of the Congo, South

Sudan, Libya, Burkina Faso, the Northern Triangle of Central America, and the decade-plus war in Syria – just to name a few – have helped drive the upward trend.[20] Moreover, the UNHCR estimates that over three-quarters of the refugees in the world today are in situations of "long-term displacement," with no return home in sight.[21]

But it is worth stating an important precursor to this discussion: the nations from which refugees are expelled are nations rich in culture, art, history, literature, and, of course, kind and loving people, some of whom we are getting to know a bit within these pages. For the purposes of this chapter's discussion – an overview of the refugee crisis – the focus will be narrowly tailored to the harms inflicted by war and disaster, rather than the countless beautiful stories of the people living in these places. Perhaps nothing is more understandably frustrating to a person with pride in her home country than to have an outsider purport to give a full picture of that country, but instead choose to focus only on the negatives. This will not be anywhere near a full picture, but rather a focus on the harms, evils, and inadequacies that unjustly spurred mass exile.

❊——❊——❊

Malak, Yasmina, and Asma are sufferers of the Syrian civil war, what is considered by the UNHCR to be "the biggest humanitarian and refugee crisis of our time."[22]

The world has watched for more than a decade while Syria has been enveloped in violence. A brief snapshot of the war and its battlelines would not do it justice: an array of domestic and international forces contribute to a brutal fight between myriad pro-regime and anti-regime groups – all while coalition efforts against ISIS and Turkish forces' operations against Syrian Kurds became intertwined in the chaos.[23] International sanctions and the national currency's depreciation have only made life in Syria even more suffocating, as many families are unable to acquire basic necessities.[24] A recent analysis reflected on the war's "descent into horror" over the previous decade, describing how deeply entangled the conflict has become since the crackdown on protests that first catalyzed it:

> The country has descended into an ever more complex civil war: jihadis promoting a Sunni theocracy have eclipsed opposition forces fighting for a democratic and pluralistic Syria, and regional powers have backed various local forces to advance their geopolitical interests on Syrian battlefields.[25]

The consequences are more clear-cut. In the midst of the war, families across the nation have lived in fear of violent attacks, bombings, gunshots, and death. Thirteen and a half million Syrians – a number greater than half of Syria's prewar population and more than the population of New York City and Los Angeles combined – have been displaced from their homes.[26] About half are internally displaced within Syria, and the other half fled the country altogether as refugees.[27] Overall, at least half of those affected by the crisis are children, like Malak at the time of her departure, who grew up knowing little other than instability.[28] And almost 80,000 Syrians have traveled across the desert in search of peace and security in Za'atari.

Over a decade of ongoing war has dealt an appalling death toll of more than 500,000 people.[29] As the UN High Commissioner for Human Rights has put it, these half a million deaths have been met with a "collective shrug" by the international community and world leaders.[30] While photos like that of Aylan temporarily captivate the world and motivate action, the emotion eventually wears off and the deaths of children and families across Syria continue on.

Many who have stayed in Syria have experienced rampant acts of violence and human rights violations. Annual reports by the international nonprofit Human Rights Watch describe them in detail, noting those committed by ISIS, the Syrian-Russian military alliance, anti-government armed groups, the US-led coalition and US-backed forces, and Turkish forces. Landmines planted by ISIS have killed and maimed individuals at random. Pro-government and anti-government groups have indiscriminately attacked neighborhoods, arbitrarily detained and tortured individuals with claims that they are partial to the other side, and sometimes interfered with attempted humanitarian aid. Chemical attacks, the majority of which have been undertaken by government forces, have choked the life from innocent civilians. Rape and sexual violence have been perpetrated in large numbers, while children have been recruited into the war as soldiers in a battle they do not understand.[31]

Beyond Syria, the world has watched as crises have developed around the world – from the Rohingya genocide in Myanmar, to instability in Central America and

Afghanistan, to famine and civil war in Somalia, to conflicts in South Sudan and Yemen, and beyond.

At the height of its violence in 2017, the genocide in Myanmar gave rise to the fastest-growing human displacement since the 1994 Rwandan genocide.[32] The Rohingya people – described by the UN Secretary-General as "one of, if not the, most discriminated people[s] in the world"[33] – have been victims of "house by house" killings by the military.[34] Though the Rohingya ethnic group has long faced discrimination and violence, 2017 saw a coordinated assault by the Myanmar government after a group of Rohingya militants launched attacks on police posts in August.[35] The UN Human Rights Council, in a 2018 report, labeled the violence against the Rohingya people "crimes against humanity," noting murders, imprisonment, torture, enslavement, and rape.[36] Human rights lawyers on the ground say that the genocide is still continuing today despite involvement by the UN.[37]

In Central America, gang intimidation and threats have become shockingly commonplace within the "Northern Triangle" nations of El Salvador, Guatemala, and Honduras. The three countries each experienced civil wars in the 1980s, leaving in their wake a number of young men without job opportunities; "a large pool of demobilized and unemployed men with easy access to weapons morphed into organized criminal groups."[38] Gangs have grown rapidly and come to effectively dominate entire regions of the Northern Triangle. The ongoing battles between gangs and government security forces attempting to control them have resulted in these nations being consistently ranked among the most violent in the world.[39] Meanwhile, the governments of El Salvador,

Guatemala, and Honduras are largely incapable of protecting citizens against these gangs; at times they are even complicit in the violence. Ultimately, then, "for too many, the only way to escape the gang[s] is to flee home altogether."[40]

Women and children in particular are victimized by the crisis. They face overwhelming rates of gang-related homicide, sexual assault, and extortion, as well as domestic violence, that the governments of the three nations are largely unable or unwilling to control.[41] The trauma that vicious gender- and sex-based threats and attacks inflict only exacerbates the issue. As one example, the UNHCR interviewed a woman named Norma who fled to the US from El Salvador. A target of gang members because her husband was a police officer, Norma had been abducted by several members and raped at a cemetery. Her account is horrifying: "They took their turns ... they tied me by the hands. They stuffed my mouth so I would not scream." And before they left: "They threw me in the trash." Determined to fight back, Norma's husband reported the monstrous crimes, but that report only increased the likelihood that she would be victimized again. Not knowing what else to do, Norma fled. From a detention center in the US in 2015, she told the UNHCR of the deep trauma she still must deal with on a day-to-day basis, on top of having to be without her family:

> I feel dirty, so very dirty. This is why I wake up not wanting to live. I feel I have sinned, and this sin lives inside me . . . . Sometimes, I wake up and think it was just a nightmare, but then I feel the pain and remember it was not.[42]

Several more crises have victimized families around the globe. In South America, political and economic instability in Venezuela has led more than five million people to be forcibly displaced since 2014;[43] Venezuela's current displaced population is now the second largest only to Syria.[44] In the Middle East beyond Syria, Afghanistan became enveloped in renewed chaos as the Taliban overtook control of the country, creating another refugee emergency almost overnight.[45] Yemen's civil war has led to food insecurity and an overwhelming number of child deaths due to malnutrition, and many Palestinian refugees remain without homes as a consequence of the Arab-Israeli conflicts.[46] In Asia beyond Myanmar, members of the Uyghur minority group are fleeing China in the face of widespread and systemic human rights and labor violations.[47] And in Africa, there is the vicious combination of drought and an ongoing civil war in Somalia, severe food shortages and prolonged violence in South Sudan, and continued conflict in the Central African Republic.[48] Burkina Faso has seen 6 percent of its population displaced in a war against militant terrorist groups, while multiple conflicts have only compounded health care challenges created by Ebola, measles, and now COVID-19 in the Democratic Republic of the Congo.[49]

The world is engulfed in a global refugee crisis the likes of which history has never seen; the exodus from Syria to Za'atari is just one scene of many.

※———※———※

For those able to escape home alive, one potential destination is the refugee camp. About six million people, or more than 20 percent of refugees, live in camps.[50] Temporary shelters for those fleeing home, and protected by international law as safe havens during war, refugee camps have long been mysterious places to observers around the world – perhaps surfacing every once in a while in the news or in Tweets by celebrities upon their humanitarian visits.[51] But little is widely discussed about where these camps are and what life is like within them.

Those living in refugee camps around the world typically fled somewhat recently. This means the largest refugee camps correspond, to a degree, with the largest of today's global conflicts and abuses; they compose a snapshot of the most suffering populations. For example, the most populated camp complex in the world, Kutupalong in Bangladesh, is a consequence of the persecution of the Rohingyas in Myanmar next door.[52] In short order, Kutupalong became a settlement of more than 700,000 people.[53] Appalling pictures exposed the world to Rohingya families desperately crossing and climbing out of the Naf River at the border between Bangladesh and Myanmar.[54]

Increasingly, however, camps do not end up being anywhere near as temporary as had once been hoped. Za'atari's ongoing existence reminds us that a camp's lifespan depends first and foremost on the establishment of peace and stability back home. Without a peaceful Syria to return to, Za'atari residents have no choice but to stay in the camp or be permanently resettled by the UN – a highly and increasingly unlikely prospect.

The thirty-year-old Dadaab camp in Kenya is another example. Most of Dadaab's residents fled Somalia in search of a modicum of hope.[55] But as a former UN Secretary-General observed:

> Even for those who reach the camps, there is often no hope. Many are simply too weak after long journeys across the arid lands and die before they can be nursed back to strength. For people who need medical attention, there are often no medicines.[56]

The uncertainty of life in Dadaab is in some ways even more pronounced than in Za'atari; the Kenyan government declared it would close the camp and require refugees to return to Somalia – only for that decision to be held unconstitutional and blocked by the nation's top court in 2017.[57] For the time being, Dadaab stands as home to more than 200,000 people.[58]

Life in refugee camps varies, and no camp is entirely typical of the experience. Most are administered by the UNHCR; as in the case of Za'atari, they are often run jointly with the hosting government.[59] As in Za'atari, there are staff and volunteers representing various international non-governmental organizations (NGOs) present at the camp, doing their best to serve the needs of the residents.

But the core system of top-down aid is inadequate in many places. The basic challenges of refugee camps mirror those in Za'atari. Refugees are often not provided sufficient in-kind or cash-based food assistance necessary to prevent malnutrition, frequently receiving less than the 2,100 calories per day goal set by the UNHCR.[60] Water shortages are an issue, particularly as many camps like Za'atari are built in deserts. UNHCR estimates indicate that over half of refugee camps "do not have enough water to fulfill the recommended 20 liters per person per day."[61] Health care is an ongoing challenge, as camps are frequently far from better-resourced facilities; this is especially problematic around the initial arrival of refugees, when the risk of death is greatest.[62] When it comes to education, only about six in ten refugee children in the world attend primary school (compared to the nine-in-ten average for all children); the issue is more acute for those living in camps and especially for girls.[63] Poor sanitation and lack of access to electricity are additional fundamental problems that compound many of the others.[64]

In part because of this insufficiency of external aid, refugees in camps take the initiative to innovatively build up economies to meet their needs.[65] Still, this is a major uphill battle as well. Frequently, as in Za'atari before 2017 when Jordan allowed Syrian refugees in camps to obtain work permits, the only formally available or permitted jobs in camps are assisting in their administration.[66] Restrictions on movement out of camps limit opportunities to find work in nearby settlements. The result is the development of informal economies of small businesses within camps, which themselves are difficult to build given refugees' limited or nonexistent capital.[67] Recently in camps including Za'atari, however, there has been a movement toward a "self-reliance" model built on cash-based aid, which has helped camp residents more easily develop markets to improve their communities' overall welfare and sense of freedom.[68]

Then there are the underlying mental health issues. Families struggle to come to terms with the loss of their loved ones, often occurring in front of their very eyes, and the new lives they are forced to lead. To deal with that trauma, without sufficient resources to support your family, with no clear path forward ... that is the challenge of a refugee camp. Still, as we will see, residents of Za'atari and other camps have fought to bring new hope and new life to the world's refugee camps.

Looking beyond camps, the majority of refugees live in cities within host nations like Jordan, where they are permitted to stay on a temporary basis. The challenges facing these refugees who are provisionally living in cities are broadly similar to those in camps. There is less of a UN and NGO support infrastructure for these refugees – meaning they are sometimes even more forgotten than refugees in camps – but they generally have more autonomy.[69]

An urgent underlying challenge is that the countries that temporarily accept refugees, whether in camps or host cities, are not the most resourced to accommodate them; developing countries host 85 percent of refugees.[70] As the UNCHR's leader described the situation, "[Displacement] continues to be a global issue, an issue for all States, but one that challenges most directly the poorer countries – not the richer countries – in spite of the rhetoric."[71] This asymmetry has been on display in the Syrian crisis, as neighboring Turkey, Jordan, Iraq, and Lebanon host more than 80 percent of Syrian refugees; Germany is the only "high-income" economy among the top five host countries for Syrians.[72]

This means refugees are most likely to be in places that are less able to provide the strong economic, educational, and health-related support systems they need. Countries that temporarily host refugees are often not willing to grant citizenship for the same reason they either do not participate in or curtail their participation in the UNHCR's permanent resettlement program: concern with already limited public resources. Their reluctance to legally permit refugees to work, which restricts refugees' ability to provide for themselves, is in part to prevent their settlement from becoming more permanent in nature.[73] Worse, the COVID-19 pandemic has disproportionately affected refugee and asylum-seeking populations, who are more prone to exclusion from economic opportunities and critical health services.[74]

For very few refugees, there is a permanent alternative: formal resettlement to new cities and towns around the world. But only a miniscule 1 percent of all refugees were resettled in 2016, and even that number has been falling significantly.[75]

The mid-twentieth-century international agreement to welcome refugees is a story of intended world unity in support of the most vulnerable among us. After years of destruction and displacement wrought by World War II and the Holocaust, global leaders came together to change what it meant to care for those without a home – to usher in a new era intended to be marked by greater compassion by promising to welcome refugees who arrived at their borders. They agreed that these "refugees" – or individuals with a well-founded fear of persecution because of race, religion, nationality, social group, or political opinion – should not be turned away, but should be welcomed in and provided certain rights. This established the legal backdrop for the refugee system we know today. With the initial agreement in 1951 and its amendment in 1967, nations around the world decided that when it comes to those who are in the deepest distress, our humanity matters more than our nationality.[76]

Playing a hybrid supervisory and operational role in the process,[77] the UNHCR "identifies the most vulnerable refugees for resettlement and then makes recommendations to select countries."[78] Ultimately, however, countries determine whether they will accept those recommendations, and shifting policies and rhetoric in Europe and the US are making it more and more unlikely that any given refugee will be resettled.

Only a small group of about thirty nations actively resettle refugees.[79] The US has historically stood out among its peers as the leading resettlement nation.[80] Since 1975, America has resettled three million refugees from around the world.[81] Between 1982 and 2016, the US welcomed 69 percent of resettled refugees, followed by Canada and Australia at 14 percent and 11 percent, respectively.[82] Emma Lazarus's poem quotation on the Statute of Liberty in New York Harbor ("Give me your tired, your poor, / Your huddled masses yearning to breathe free, / The wretched refuse of your teeming shore. / Send these, the homeless, tempest-tost to me, / I lift my lamp beside the golden door!") has stood as a beacon of acceptance of those who are the most unprotected in the world.[83]

But that changed in recent years under the Trump administration. America's intake of refugees dramatically declined, as the numbers of refugees resettled in the US went down from 92,000 to 33,000 from 2016 to 2017,[84] and down again to a low of fewer than 12,000 in 2020.[85] The US resettled a startlingly low 62 refugees from Syria in 2018, a decline from 12,587 two years prior.[86] This drop drove a major overall plunge in refugee resettlements, meaning the odds of any given refugee being brought to live permanently in a stable country became even more minute. Moreover, this occurred at a time when COVID-19 further limited safety outlets for refugees; at the early height of the pandemic, 168 nations "fully or partially closed their borders, with around 90 making no exception for those seeking asylum. Some . . . pushed asylum seekers, including children, back to their countries of origin."[87] Altogether, then, 2020 saw historic lows for global refugee resettlement, meaning the resettlement of even less than 1 percent of refugees.[88] So, just as refugees in camps like Za'atari and nearby host communities in Jordan cannot count on peace at home, they sadly cannot count on permanent resettlement either.

※———※———※

We are left with a grim picture of the state of affairs facing refugees: we are in the midst of a historic global refugee crisis, without an immediate path to permanent living solutions for refugee families. A report by the Council on Foreign Relations provides an apt summary:

> Wars, persecution, and instability have driven the number of refugees to historic highs. Rather than offer protection, many countries have erected new barriers, leaving many of today's refugees in protracted limbo . . . . The international refugee regime . . . has proven adept at providing life-saving assistance in response to emergencies but has been challenged to provide meaningful opportunities for the long-term displaced or support the communities hosting them. Compounding the challenges it faces is the retreat of many advanced democracies amid rising anti-immigrant sentiment.[89]

As Mohamed, a Somali refugee in the Kakuma camp in Kenya who has waited twenty years for resettlement, lamented in an interview: "It surprises me that money and capital move around the world in seconds, but it takes a refugee decades . . . for a place to call home."[90]

All the while, life goes on for refugees like Yasmina, Malak, and Asma in places like Za'atari. Despite the darkness they have faced, they consistently find it within themselves to bring forth their own sparks of hope, compassion, and inspiration. Toward those sparks is where we will follow them next.

Part II

Spark

But I know, somehow, that only when it is dark enough can you see the stars.
—Dr. Martin Luther King, Jr.,
"I've Been to the Mountaintop"

CHAPTER 5

New Beginnings

Asma could barely sleep in her tent that night. Not because the scorching Za'atari heat makes her sheets annoyingly sticky, though that certainly didn't help. But because it was the eve of the day she had been awaiting for weeks: teacher training day.

A Jordan-based NGO called We Love Reading was offering an opportunity to train teachers of young children. Its staff had been posting notices and spreading the word around the camp. Interested potential teachers should arrive at the training center at eight o'clock in the morning to receive their materials and complete a brief orientation.

It was as if, somehow, during the worst period of Asma's life as her child had recently passed away, there was a renewed sense of potential in miserable Za'atari. Something inside her awakened for the first time since leaving Dara'a. Asma remembered her love for school, reading in the dark back at home until she could no longer keep her eyes open. Sleeping in her uniform. Rushing to school each day.

Still, she also remembered other things.

She remembered her insecurity whenever a teacher asked a question. She remembered how, though she had vividly dreamt of being a teacher when she was a child, she was extremely shy despite desiring to speak up. And she knew that she had not overcome that lack of confidence in the past few years.

But, after the loss of her child, Asma had told herself she would do everything within her power to ensure all children in Za'atari received the love they deserved. Every precious child. She had missed the opportunity to be a teacher in Dara'a; now was her opportunity in Za'atari.

This morning, in fact. At dawn, Asma woke up and walked swiftly to the training center. She arrived first and was at the head of the line in front of the door. Shortly after eight o'clock, an older woman came to the door with a name tag: Rana. She smiled politely at Asma and let her and her followers into the building. The meeting began.

"I was afraid that she would ask me about my education, because [I thought] all of the others had college degrees – and I did not."

Rana, who was the NGO's founder, gave a presentation on the teaching program. Asma could hardly pay attention, still unsure if she would be eligible. At the end, it was time for the would-be teachers to formally register and receive their teaching materials at the front of the room. Asma walked up gently, feeling certain that her lack of credentials – her time lost – would halt her second chance at this dream.

"But when I went up to the front, they only asked me for my name. They gave me a book bag full of children's storybooks. I was so happy."

That night, Asma, like she had many years ago as a girl in Dara'a, read books for hours on end. This time they were children's stories meant to uplift the next generation in Za'atari.

"I was reading those books all the time. I even put them beside me on the bed while I was sleeping."

Her childhood dream from Dara'a could possibly be recaptured, albeit in a much different place, in the wake of an unthinkable tragedy. Still, she was ready. "I told myself:

"Andee amal."

"I have hope."

——————*

"Hold out a bit longer," Yasmina would tell herself. This life – of tents, morning bread rations, dust, lack of water, and loneliness – was not the life of her past, and it was not to be her future.

But heading home was not an option ... yet. Yasmina would get updates from her family members, friends, and former clients back in Dara'a about the status of life in Syria. Some of her close relatives had returned to Dara'a, so, like many residents of Za'atari with loved ones back home, she had direct insight. She would talk on the phone regularly with them.

As she waited to hear news of peace back home, she could not find it within herself to start life anew, to establish a shop in Za'atari. Even as weddings were a part of the fabric of life in Za'atari – people were still getting married, after all – she resisted the instinct to put her wedding preparation skills to use. Her shop was still upright back in Dara'a, Yasmina thought, and she would one day reopen it with all her old customers returning over time. Starting a business in Za'atari would mean forsaking that hope of home, and, more practically, using precious resources on an endeavor that would not last.

Even when her cousin announced her engagement, Yasmina was reluctant to get involved. But her cousin insisted: "Yasmina, only you can do my hairdressing! My hair is your problem, not my problem. You have to take care of me!" Yasmina acquiesced, to rave reviews from her cousin's family and the wedding guests. Her cousin was grateful, and some of the spirit of her Dara'a shop was reignited inside Yasmina. Not enough, however, to take the plunge into a new life in Za'atari.

But at around the same time, it became clear that she had to do something: she had no choice in the matter but to innovate. The funds her husband earned from his job supporting NGOs' aid efforts in the camp, plus the family's daily rations, were simply not enough. "I had to work and help my husband put food on the table."

Adding to her burden, Yasmina received news she had been dreading. Through calls with her relatives back in Dara'a, she learned that her family's house had been destroyed.

So while Yasmina wanted desperately to return to Dara'a soon, it was at that moment that she knew should could not. "No. I could not go back to Syria. I lost everything . . . even my house."

With her family's support, she started doing some work from her trailer in Za'atari. "My sisters and my cousins encouraged me, and I started to do hairdressing from home." Then, Yasmina made a monumental decision. She parted with the only items of monetary value she had – and her most precious memories of home and her own wedding day – for startup capital to launch a salon and wedding shop in Za'atari: "I sold my gold necklace, rings, and bracelet."

"It was scary because I was afraid that after opening my salon, I would end up going back home. It was difficult. Frightening."

She used the first bit of that money to rent two plain white wedding dresses from a dressmaker in Jordan. There was no looking back. Yasmina the wedding master had arrived in Za'atari. The "Salon of Lights" was born.

❋ —— ❋ —— ❋

Malak was two years into camp life and still just a teenager. Two years without schooling, in a new place far from home, with a small fraction of the resources and comforts she had back in Damascus.

Malak used that time to become an artist.

Like many entrepreneurs, Malak had to be scrappy about the way she improved her skills. During those two years, she had no one to teach her art – no art history courses to give her context, no hands-on training to show her different approaches, and no mentors to guide her on how to start a studio. With YouTube videos as guidance, the minimal supplies she brought from Damascus, and the external metal walls of her home trailer as a canvas, she made do with what she had. Malak's dad, himself a talented artist though he never pursued art professionally, was always supporting her. "When my dad saw that I could draw well and that it motivated me, he started to pay attention to what I was doing, to what pictures I was drawing."[1]

Malak drew and painted what was in her heart. But the sometimes-somber tone of her art caused some concern among family and friends. This was the case with one of her favorite pieces: a charcoal drawing of a rugged-looking man with a stoic face and a half-shaven beard. To many, it appeared ominous and disturbing ... a sign that Malak was not her normal joyful self. But for Malak, art was a natural outlet for both the good and the bad feelings inside her. "All my paintings and drawings tell stories and express my feelings. Some people would say that my art communicated to them that I am sad. I don't mean it that way; I'm just telling my story."

Eventually, Malak was able to become engaged in an educational program run by an NGO; Za'atari residents called it the "Arabic Center." The Arabic Center would bring together all of Malak's building blocks: the confidence that she could become an artist, the best friend to encourage her to reach new heights, and the manager to organize her launch.

Like back in Damascus, Malak found herself drawn to specific classes – really any classes that involved any kind of art. And there was, much to her delight, one teacher at the Arabic Center who would always hang his paintings on the walls of his classroom. Malak approached the teacher to tell him of their common interest. "I saw a teacher who was always drawing pictures. I liked his art, so I told him that I, too, like to draw." The teacher was intrigued, so he asked to see some of her work. Never unprepared, Malak had a few pieces of art with her in her backpack. She showed him the charcoal drawing of the half-shaven man, along with a few paintings she had been working on. "I told him that my drawings are not that good. They're not perfect. But he said, 'No, you draw very well and you have a skill for mixing colors together well. Not everyone can do that.'"[2] The teacher then examined Malak further: "So he started to test my ability by asking me to match different colors, and I got them perfectly." He invited her to join a group of artists in the camp called the Za'atari Art Committee and to put her paintings in a new Za'atari gallery. These were just the seeds of encouragement Malak needed.

But art was not the only thing that inspired Malak. Debate did as well. After so much time thinking and reflecting about the issues surrounding her life – the Arab Spring, the war in Syria, the Za'atari camp and the refugee crisis, children's and women's rights, and now her future and the future of her generation – Malak was eager to talk about those issues with her peers. She decided that she was called to be a leader ... someone who would build up the Za'atari community.

In one fateful debate class, Malak was going toe-to-toe with another girl – about what exactly, she does not remember. "I met Roaa the first time," Malak laughs, "because we were arguing. We were fighting each other."

When the two peers left class, they walked in the same direction, southwest toward the lower districts. Then, as other students broke off, Malak and Roaa kept walking together. Eventually, the debate combatants discovered that they were also neighbors. That walk home was the beginning of the closest friendship in each of their lives.

Over time, with her teacher's training and Roaa's encouragement, Malak decided she would begin developing the art studio she had always dreamt of. Roaa would manage it. After a trip to Amman to purchase art supplies, she set up a makeshift studio in the corner of the bedroom shared with her older sister Hoda. A floor-standing easel and a chair were placed against the window, paint tubes were lined up across the floor, and her framed paintings were posted against the wall. Hoda, enlivened by her little sister's renewed spark, was thrilled to see their room awakened by art.

To Malak, this is what the charcoal drawing of the half-shaven man was all about. Though many saw the drawing as depressing, Malak saw it as primarily hopeful. The man's stoic face may have represented pain, yes, but it also represented determination and a clean start. His eyes were cast forward as he shaved, contemplating the opportunities of the future. Malak fittingly titled the painting "New Beginnings." There were bittersweet feelings in her heart as she reflected on her life back in Damascus, but there was also optimism for a shot at something new – excitement about commencing another chapter in her life. Now, with her friend and to-be-manager Roaa, with her encouraging parents, with her supportive teacher, and with her sister

Hoda sacrificing her personal space for the cause, Malak had much to look forward to. That's not something she could have imagined during those first painful nights in Za'atari.

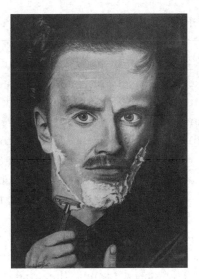

————*

It is a common piece of wisdom given to aspiring entrepreneurs: try to think of difficult experiences as catalysts, as opportunities. As Phil Knight, the cofounder of Nike, put it: "When you see only problems, you're not seeing clearly."[3] Conan O'Brien, longtime late-night host and founder of his television production firm, spoke to graduating students at Dartmouth College about the potential to transform "misfortune" into "profound reinvention."[4] The late Steve Jobs, founder of Apple, famously said in 1995: "I'm convinced that about half of what separates the successful entrepreneurs from the non-successful ones is pure perseverance."[5]

But the entrepreneurs in Za'atari were not just experiencing "problems"; they were living through the greatest crisis in recent history. The destruction of their homes and their subsequent displacement to a refugee camp were "misfortunes" of the most difficult kind, and it would take more than mere "perseverance" to survive, much less to start successful businesses. Their scars are countless times more severe than what their counterparts in Silicon Valley can imagine on their worst days. The business schools at Stanford and Harvard do not prepare students for this in their entrepreneurship courses.

Due to forces beyond their control, the Za'atari entrepreneurs faced their worlds being turned entirely upside down. They faced trauma: the separation from and often death of their loved ones. They faced homelessness: leaving their homes to settle in a refugee camp completely unknown to them. They faced life-threatening instability: not knowing whether there would be enough food for their families, or whether anyone would be able to treat their health care needs. General entrepreneurial advice is helpful in spirit, but entrepreneurship in Za'atari involves a different level of intensity, commitment, strength, and support.

Still, perhaps with greater pain, the hope that emerges is that much more powerful – and the entrepreneurs who emerge that much more inspiring. Lights shine brightest in the darkness, and as Dr. Martin Luther King, Jr., said during his final, historic speech at Mason Temple in Memphis, Tennessee: "[O]nly when it is dark enough can you see the stars."[6]

Yasmina, Malak, Asma, and their fellow Za'atari residents had been through unthinkable pain. There was no playbook for starting over with such an austere blank slate. For these three women, there was no choice but to fight through the pain and to design new opportunities on the path in front of them. As Syrian poet Amineh Abou Kerech wrote as a thirteen-year-old, there is no instruction manual for how to create a new life, especially in times of such devastation and uncertainty:

> Can anyone teach me
> how to make a homeland?
> Heartfelt thanks if you can,
> heartiest thanks,
> from the house-sparrows,
> the apple-trees of Syria,
> and yours very sincerely.[7]

Nonetheless, the trio set about that mission to "make a homeland." Malak, though she once dreaded the idea of living in a refugee camp, would begin seeing Za'atari as a blank canvas upon which to paint her life. Yasmina would try to move past, at least for a time, the three decades of life she built in Dara'a and see Za'atari as her new community to serve. And Asma would strive to somehow transform the gravest of pains – the death of her child – into meaning and life for other children.

All three found the spark within them amidst the most terrifying nights, and that – that moment of finding faith, hope, love, and creativity despite the sadness they faced – is the most entrepreneurial thing imaginable.

CHAPTER 6

Khatwa, Khatwa

A woman in a lavender dress and matching headscarf, chasing children around her neighborhood, across the narrow gravel streets and sometimes right into their homes. A curious sight in Za'atari.

"Come listen to a story," Asma would tell them, calmly at first, when they walked by her trailer. When they would inevitably reply that they could not – often because they had work to do for their parents – her sales pitch would kick into overdrive. She would implore them, telling them that the work could wait, that their education was most important. When the children were still reluctant, she would resort to running after them. Literally chasing them. Asma would get her first "customers" any way she could.

Parents were concerned at first. Who was this mad-woman running after their children? But Asma didn't care about appearing strange; the children would come around, she thought, and the parents would react positively to the impact her new storytelling initiative would have on their kids. The program would follow a regular format: Asma reading a carefully curated story to the children, then leading an activity focused on personal growth and reading, writing, communication, and creative skills development.

Rewinding a bit, it had taken a lot for Asma to even get to the point of chasing. She had worked up the courage to attend the teacher training, yes, and she had been given an opportunity to live out her dream of teaching children. But this did not automatically wipe away her prior self-doubt. She was taking a leap of faith and committing to an uncertain process of self-growth, because she wanted so badly to support the growth of the children around her.

So Asma practiced and practiced and practiced her storytelling. Luckily, Tamara and Maya were always Asma's number one fans. Her go-to story for practicing her craft was a children's classic, with a fitting theme: "Khatwa, Khatwa" – "Step by Step." She would rehearse at home in front of Tamara and Maya, as well as her young niece.

For Asma, the key was being bold in her storytelling. She was never one to be outspoken or loud, but engaging the children – especially those who were often distracted in the first place – would have to mean *entertaining* them. It would have to mean going outside of her comfort zone to immerse them in the stories she told. "I had to practice reading the stories as if I were acting, changing my voice as I spoke."

Khatwa, Khatwa.

Engaging the children would also mean creating a storybook atmosphere in her trailer. A magical hideout for the children. So Asma began renovating the inside of the main, rectangular room in her trailer. She found long, flat, dark brown cushions to match the carpet of the room and placed them against each of the four walls. She hung baby-blue-colored flowers on the walls, and adjusted the window blinds to dim the outside light. To complete the magical ambiance, she placed a sign right near the entrance – right where the kids would look after taking off their shoes and entering – announcing the name of the storytelling initiative: "قصص للشمس," "Stories of the Sun."

Khatwa, Khatwa.

Finally, engaging the children would mean sharing stories that resonated with their experiences. Among the books she received from Rana and the We Love Reading staff, she selected a few that were the most uplifting and that connected the most with the lives of Za'atari children. Children who had witnessed war, violence, separated families, and in some cases deaths. Children who were worried about their futures or considering giving up on their ambitions.

It was with those books in hand and confidence from her practice sessions with family that Asma felt ready to reach out to the children in her neighborhood. "I went to the children on our street, door to door, with a lot of storybooks. I started to give books to them." Asma would ask the children to bring the books back to her trailer when they were finished with them, starting what was perhaps Za'atari's first community library.

"I thought that they would not bring them back, but they did." Soon, the parents began accepting the new project, especially when they saw Asma's heart for and bond with the children. "When the parents saw the children with me, they began to open the door more willingly and accept the books." The relationships had been built and the seeds had been planted for Asma's storytelling initiative.

Maybe, Asma thought, she was on to something.

✻ —— ✻ —— ✻

Asma was not the only one going against the grain in a newly emerging Za'atari still trying to find its identity. Za'atari entrepreneurs face all of the obstacles that entrepreneurs around the world face, only in a far more dramatic fashion. This was especially true for the innovators trailblazing in the earlier days of entrepreneurship in the camp, when starting businesses was not so common.

Yasmina, however, did have the benefit of experience. She could lean on the wealth of knowledge she had gained from her successful salon and wedding shop back in Dara'a. She had years of practice with makeup and hairdressing, she could explain in detail the types of wedding dresses Syrian brides loved, and she had an established style of engaging customers that worked well for her. So Yasmina had a certain confidence about her as she dove into her new startup. Moreover, love and family life did not suddenly end when the war started; Za'atari residents did not need to be convinced to proceed with their weddings, even with the uncertainty and strife surrounding their lives.

Still, Za'atari was a totally new economy, one closed off from the rest of the world by concrete walls and security guards. Yasmina's first challenge was figuring out her supply chain. Her first two rented dresses were paid for with the money she made from selling her rings, bracelet, and necklace. And her first supplier was a merchant she met on a shopping trip to Amman. "When I started my salon, I went to buy something from a gentleman from Jordan. After two rentals, we got to know each other and he started to help me."

With those two dresses, Yasmina launched the salon from her home: her family's trailer in District 3. Her first customers came from her personal network – those who attended her cousin's wedding or who remembered her store from back in Dara'a. Things were slow in those early days, which allowed her to generate complementary income by sewing her own dresses and selling them back to her new business partner in Amman.

The slower pace allowed Yasmina to refamiliarize herself with her craft and to build her team. By then, after years of experience back in Dara'a, Yasmina knew and cherished her role. "I design the brides' hair and makeup, and then handle their dresses [both for engagements and for weddings] . . . . I especially feel joy when I see my clients in the dresses I get, or make, for them." As for recruiting staff, she was uncertain she would be able to find anyone willing to take the plunge into her new venture alongside her. But in this case, fate intervened. One day, Yasmina heard an unexpected knock on her trailer's door. She opened it and looked up to see a teenage girl who was taller than her. With a nervous smile on her face, the girl shyly said hello. She said her name was Mona and asked if she could work for Yasmina on a part-time basis. Her parents were comfortable with it, she quickly noted – an important assurance because, though women's participation in the labor force was much more frequent in the camp (in part thanks to role models like Yasmina, Asma, and Malak), it was not as common back home.[1] Seeing this young woman as a godsend, Yasmina accepted her offer with no questions asked.

Mona would come to manage engagement with clients. This was no small responsibility; in fact, supporting and reassuring clients was perhaps the biggest challenge facing the Salon of Lights. Many would be stressed about their big days. Some would be unable to pay. With an uncontrollable laugh, Yasmina remembers one incident involving a particularly problematic client:

"One time I made a dress for a bride and everyone loved it. Everyone said she was beautiful ... except for her aunt, that is, who felt the dress was not how she had wanted it to be."

The wedding day arrived, but Yasmina sensed the disagreement with the aunt would not end so easily. Four hours into the proceedings, her phone rang. "She called me and said, 'We didn't like your work, so we won't be paying you. The bride here is very sad. She has locked herself in the back room and won't come out. The wedding is ruined.'"

Uncertain of what to do, Yasmina patiently tried to reason with the aunt on the phone. But Mona ... Mona would not take this sitting down. Despite her initial timidity, she had begun to lean into her true personality as she worked as Yasmina's apprentice: bold, charismatic, and with an ever-present sense of humor.

"[Mona] is young and has a strong personality. She didn't like what she heard, so she actually walked right over to the wedding." When she arrived, unannounced and uninvited, Mona discovered that the aunt had been a bit ... misleading. Not only was the bride not locked in a room in disappointment, she was dancing and celebrating at the center of the party. So, as Yasmina recalls, Mona confronted the aunt directly:

"She told the aunt, 'Look, the bride is happy, and you are going to pay for the dress ... or I will take it with me.'"

Back at her trailer, Yasmina received another call: "The aunt called and said, 'Yasmina, listen, I was joking with you. Everyone said the bride was so beautiful. Thank you so much for your work!'"

Mona's approach at that wedding was a tone-setter for the Yasmina-Mona duo in the future. The only remaining question: What would Mona have done if the aunt still resisted payment? Surely she would not have *really* taken the dress ... or would she have?

Yasmina smiles, with a look that says not to mess with her understudy: "Eah!" "Of course!"

──※──

Malak faced a fundamental challenge: figuring out a way to make art matter in Za'atari.

Amidst all the challenges in the camp, art took a back seat. The limited resources in Za'atari were geared toward food, housing, health, and education – meeting critical needs. So Malak's desire to launch a Za'atari-based art studio was not exactly on the expected path forward. The resources to support her were limited, and there was no real art market in the camp, as residents were usually forced to forego nonessential goods and services.

Moreover, and more personally, Malak knew she had to make the most of every opportunity she had to lift up her own family. Given this understandable lack of a market for art in Za'atari, it was not clear how her work would enable her to earn money to sustain herself and support her family when they needed it. Focusing all or most of her time on art would mean taking a risk that would affect her and her loved ones. She could not in good conscience pursue such a risk.

In the world of entrepreneurship, people regularly celebrate the entrepreneurs who take major risks in starting their businesses or in making certain management decisions. But sometimes the reality is that those risks are not as extreme as they seem; many of these entrepreneurs already have the financial stability, networks, funding support, and backup options that make even the worst-case scenario – failure, especially after a significant investment of time and resources – not truly that bad. As a result, we tend to celebrate those who are already privileged enough to venture into the unknown with the comfort of knowing that their families and futures were never genuinely at risk if they were to fail.

In Za'atari, the calculations could not be more radically different. There is no such thing as financial security, not remotely. There is often no backup option to generate income. As in Yasmina's case, the risk was extreme and as real as it gets: selling the only items of monetary value she owned to try to get her startup off the ground.

In Malak's case, she was still very young, blessed to have the option to continue schooling and not need to drop out to help her parents. She saw in front of her the opportunity to develop a career with a more established path toward sustainable income, which could be significantly helpful to her family. If she had the kind of financial stability or inbuilt backup options of more advantaged youths, perhaps she would study art in school and pursue it fully. But with the hand she was dealt, art would have to continue as a side project, at least for a time.

When more schooling options presented themselves in Za'atari, Malak finally returned to high school after a two-year break. She wanted to focus: "I stopped drawing until I finished high school." Thankfully, she had harbored a second passion since childhood: medicine. It was a passion that could potentially secure her future financially. While in high school, she identified a possible first step on the path to a career in medicine: a scholarship opportunity to attend a Jordanian university called the DAFI Tertiary Scholarship Programme, also known as the Albert Einstein German Academic Refugee Initiative scholarship program. The program was designed specifically for refugee students seeking to earn undergraduate degrees in their host nations, or their original home nations if they are able to return.[2]

"On the internet, I saw a lot of different organizations offering scholarships, so I applied. In the interview [for the DAFI Scholarship], [the interviewers] asked me what I'd like to be in the future. I said that I want to study medicine as my career – that from when I was little, I loved medicine and was interested in medical tools. Meanwhile, my art is my way of expressing myself."

After the interviews and a lull of waiting, Malak finally received the good news she had been waiting for: she had been awarded the DAFI Scholarship and accepted to Zarqa University, in the Jordanian town of Zarqa, to pursue a career in medical analysis. Then she got more good news: Roaa received the same scholarship, and had been placed in the same exact program. The two best friends, classmates, and neighbors would remain joined at the hip. "I really love the scholarship. When they accepted me, it was the best day of my life in the Za'atari camp .... . DAFI colored my life."

At this point, as she prepared for the rigors of college, she never thought art would make a resurgence in her life. Medical analysis is a difficult concentration, and her schedule would be tight. Still, every day when she and Roaa made the commute by bus to Zarqa, she would pack some art supplies – just like she did the day she was forced to leave Damascus. Just in case there might be a bit of time to pursue her first love.

$$ *\!\!—\!\!*\!\!—\!\!* $$

Za'atari's founders and CEOs face – and faced especially in the early years – a whole set of roadblocks that those in better resourced communities are fortunate to never even have to consider.

The challenge before the early Za'atari entrepreneurs is hard to overstate. Having just fled an unexpected war that drove them out of their homes, they found themselves in not just a new place, but a totally undeveloped place. An experiment. No bedrock institutions, like universities or governmental organizations, to turn to. No established markets. No banks to offer loans. Thick walls guarded by security ensuring that entry and exit – by customers, distributors, advisors, lenders – was limited.

And, outside of their ventures, Za'atari entrepreneurs' critical needs persisted. Handling their personal, family, and community circumstances itself was a daunting task. Adding a startup on top of those stresses seems nearly impossible.

Health care challenges, in particular, created an obstacle for those seeking to start businesses in Za'atari. This is especially the case for those injured in the war or with family members who needed treatment. Malwa, who was a cell phone repairman back in Dara'a, dealt with health care issues as he began launching his new cell phone repair shop in the camp. He had secured a trailer in a fantastic location right on the main road of Za'atari, officially called "Market Street," for his shop.

Malwa brought as many supplies as he could from his store back home in Dara'a – various smartphone cases and batteries, a microscope, the metal tools required – and his business started off well. But not long after he arrived in Za'atari, his son began struggling with recurring health problems. The nearest hospital at the time was far from his center of operations, so he would run back and forth throughout the day between the hospital and his shop. "I thought to myself, 'If this [routine] continues, I'm going to be the one in the hospital.'" So Malwa had to sacrifice his startup's prime location and risk the customer base he had built, and set up shop entirely anew – this time closer to the hospital. It was a difficult mid-launch transition that cost him in customers and in time, but it was necessary to support his son.[3]

For entrepreneurs with disabilities in Za'atari, the challenge is even greater. Again, it was tougher in the initial days, when many newly settled residents dealt with critical injuries stemming from the war. Eman was a girl in Dara'a when she experienced the brutality of the conflict firsthand. As she shared with Save the Children staff: "I was young when the war started in Syria. All I remember [from my injury] was that there was a lot of noise and a strong quake that shook our house. My sister and I ran to leave. We were both injured, and I lost my leg."[4]

Eman, like many youths in Za'atari, was an unaccompanied child when she arrived. Her sister came with her to Za'atari, leaving the rest of their family behind. When they got to the camp, Eman was fortunate to have been taken to a nearby Jordanian hospital for emergency care. "I had an operation on my foot. And I thought, 'This is it. I cannot walk or go to school and I will not be able to do anything. I was very sad.'" But the hospital conducted a successful surgery and helped Eman to walk again. "They put on an artificial leg that changed my life ... and all my bad thoughts went away."[5]

Eman, with a newfound hope, would set her vision on becoming a social entrepreneur who would help others in situations like hers. Accessibility issues in the camp meant people with mobility impairments were mostly forced to stay in their homes. The most common mode of transportation in Za'atari – the bikes whizzing around the camp throughout the day – was not an option for Eman and others with similar disabilities. Eman sought to provide a means of autonomy and social engagement, so she designed a new type of accessible bike created specifically for Za'atari. In the process, she would bravely battle the stigma of disability – a challenge in Za'atari, back in Dara'a, and in most if not all places in the world – and her own limitations in an inaccessible camp.[6]

Beyond the physical pain, the lasting mental and emotional effects of war create obstacles for aspiring entrepreneurs and for the people they seek to reach in their communities. Malwa was challenged every day striving to succeed as an entrepreneur while worrying constantly about the health of his son and the resources that were being provided to treat him. But through that difficulty he would access a new side of himself for his clients: he saw himself as a counselor of sorts. Each day, clients would come to him to fix their phones, passing them to him through the slim opening beneath his plexiglass window at the shop's front desk. Malwa would get to work on the phones with a variety of tools, but he would also engage his clients in conversation as they waited. How was the family back in Syria? Were you able to get a trailer here? What have you heard of the war's status? How are you feeling? For those who visited his store, what started as a simple errand would end with a sense of community and shared struggle. Creating these moments of unity and comfort became an invaluable part of Malwa's role.

Similarly, Asma was in many ways still mentally and emotionally grappling with her own loss. But she would seek to be a social entrepreneur who channeled her pain into joy and confidence for the children around her. It was the loss of her child and her journey of healing that intensified her empathy and desire to serve the children in Za'atari – and gave her a deeper connection to them.

But as she launched Stories of the Sun in her newly renovated trailer, Asma quickly began to see how challenging her mission would be. How deep the effects of war can run.

She remembers one moment in particular that taught her how far she and the Za'atari community would have to go to undo the damaging effects of war on their children. During her first storytelling session with nonfamily members – her first real, non-preparatory session – she brought crayons and construction paper for the children. After reading a brief story to them, she distributed a sheet of paper to each child and placed the crayons in the center of the room on the carpet.

Asma asked the children, all seated on the ground in a semicircle around her, to draw pictures of anything in their minds – to express themselves however they wanted, to empty what was in their hearts and imaginations. When she stood to stroll around and see what they had come up with, she was taken aback by what she saw. As she passed from one drawing to another, it became clear that what was on their minds was what no child should ever have to think about: war.

"They all drew soldiers and war equipment."

Asma understood it. What else could a child exposed to brutal violence so early in life be thinking about?

But even in the middle of such a sobering moment, there was a ray of light. One drawing in the group was different. The artist's name was Nawara – or "light" in Arabic. The smallest girl in the class. When Asma peered over Nawara's shoulder to look at her drawing, expecting to see a tank or a fighter plane, her hope was revived.

It was a drawing of a red rose. A drawing of love in the midst of fifteen drawings of war.

Asma was heartened. There would be progress over time.

Khatwa, Khatwa.

CHAPTER 7

Balloons

With the Eid holiday upon them, the wise Yasmina and dynamic Mona emerged as quite the entrepreneurial duo.

Eid was the busiest time for weddings. Many potential clients were in play for Yasmina and Mona. Brides-to-be would ask their families, friends, and neighbors who to go to in this new place to prepare them for their big days. Word slowly began to spread around Za'atari about Yasmina, who was still operating out of her home trailer. Word-of-mouth referrals, stemming both from her work back in Dara'a and her initial work in Za'atari, became the strongest marketing tool for the Salon of Lights.

"It was hard at first, but gradually things started to improve. When people saw my work, they began to recommend me to their families and friends."

Beyond the duo's attention to detail, sense for beautiful hair and dress designs, and organizational acuity was one key ingredient: a warmth and gentle kindness that ensured their clients would rave to their families and friends about them. As Yasmina describes it: "I like to treat my customers like I treat my own family. I meet them with a smile and am happy to see them, and I help them choose what they like. It makes them feel like they are in their own homes."

Being entrusted with the responsibility of preparing someone for her wedding day is a major deal, and Yasmina took it seriously. From the moment a prospective client would come to her front door, Yasmina would strive to ensure that the bride-to-be felt fully taken care of. And, recognizing Yasmina's wisdom and skill, her clients would put complete trust in her. Yasmina fondly remembers one client who trusted her so much that she absolutely refused to look at herself in the mirror before the wedding; she knew her hair, makeup, and dress were in good hands. She did not want to even think about them.

All this time, Yasmina was running operations in her home. With more clients exhibiting that type of trust, loving their weddings, and spreading the word about Yasmina and Mona, the demand for their services grew to a point where they needed to scale up to a dedicated shop. Gone were the days of only two rented plain white dresses. Now the duo was working with a larger inventory and multiple clients at a time, so they needed a bigger trailer with a spacious salon and a room to showcase their wide variety of dresses.

From her experience in Dara'a, Yasmina knew location was key. There are two main business roads in Za'atari: Market Street and Saudi Market. Thankfully, she was able to acquire a spot right in the center of Saudi Market. It was an extended trailer with two components to it: a long, narrow room that ended with a slim door to a more expansive room in the back. Yasmina and Mona's first couple of years of work had generated enough profit to lavishly decorate the store, so they did just that.

The aluminum trailer, once empty with plain walls, was transformed into perhaps the most vibrant store in all of Za'atari, if not Jordan. A vertical wooden sign now stood by the front window to identify the pink-walled salon, as did a horizontal white one placed on the front shingles. There was a small porch, where a sparkling emerald green dress hung from the ceiling to mark the entryway. The spacious back room was a quiet, private beauty salon with two brown leather seats facing mirrors that reached the ceiling. This is where the bulk of brides' preparation would take place. It is where they would rest and drink tea with Yasmina and Mona, and it would also function as a lab where Yasmina would design and create dresses of her own.

To complement the simple and serene salon, the duo would transform the first room into an extravagant showroom, hanging twenty dresses from the ceiling with barely any breathing room between them. A client walking in would feel almost like she was entering a magnificent forest of dresses, as she waded through vibrant colors, sparkles, glitters, and soft fabrics. As Asma's trailer would elicit a magical aura for her children, Yasmina's would elicit an aura of uncompromising celebration for her clients and their family members.

The new space was a second marketing boon for Yasmina and Mona. No longer relying only on word of mouth, the new store was a colorful attention-grabber for all residents walking or biking through the bustling Saudi Market.

"Step by step, my salon started to grow." Step by Step. Khatwa, Khatwa.

The growth of the shop's client base was not limited to just Za'atari: to Yasmina's surprise, others outside the camp came calling. Syrian brides-to-be in host communities in Amman and other Jordanian cities had heard of her work and requested the Salon of Lights's services. This became a sort of ambassadorial role, on behalf of Syria and Za'atari, in two ways. First, Yasmina loved the idea of helping Syrians living within different Jordanian communities shine brightly on their big days. "When I see the dresses I make being worn by the Syrian brides, I feel proud." And second, Syrians and Jordanians outside the camp would often be surprised to learn Yasmina was doing business in Za'atari and that there are weddings in the camp. They sometimes looked down on the camp and its people, and carried prejudices against them. Yasmina's response: "This is a city like any place else."

As one of the founders and matriarchs of the salon and wedding preparation industry in Za'atari, Yasmina realized she was fueling a bit of a movement. For anyone who thought that elaborate, high-quality wedding celebrations were not going to be the norm in Za'atari, Yasmina's work helped dispel that notion quickly. As weddings became more commonplace in Za'atari, competition rose. New wedding shops popped up in the camp, from trailers throughout Market Street and Saudi Market to home-based shops in several districts.

Yasmina only smiles at the thought of this as "competition." She is delighted about the level of celebration in Za'atari. She never says her store is better or her dresses more striking or her client service more attentive. Given everything she has been through thus far, it takes much more than a rival store to rock Yasmina's faith.

"Every store has its own way. Everyone is different, and God will provide. At the end, what God wants will happen."

The same thing that Yasmina had in great abundance in starting this venture is what would sustain it, and keep her grounded during difficult times:

"Iman."

"Faith."

————*

Part of being an entrepreneur is being on the lookout for opportunities, even when you have limited bandwidth. For Malak, university was the focus – and it took significant effort. "Medical analysis courses are very difficult and there was a lot of pressure on me." She had mentally resigned to the idea that art would take a back seat in her life during her studies. "I never thought I could improve my art."

Nevertheless, just like during her early days in Za'atari, art made its way into her life. Through art, she was able to channel her stresses into creativity. "That pressure [of college] turned me to art. Art helped me empty out all that energy . . . . When I had an exam, I would have to draw."

Though she had no intentions of honing her craft, Malak improved dramatically in the heat of the academic years at Zarqa University. "Before college, my art was average; it was not as beautiful as it is now. I was not at this level. Right when I started college, I improved a lot." There was not much formal training available, so Malak used online learning tools like she had previously in the camp. "I was always watching a lot of videos. I did not go to any classes to learn. I learned from practice."

The blessing of not having teachers or structured classes is that Malak developed her own unique style without being constrained by others' ideas of what "good art" looks like. "My model is myself," she says with a smile.

Malak experimented with different artistic styles and mediums. "In elementary school, I used pencils. Then I moved up to watercolors, then to acrylic. As I got to higher skill levels, I started creating oil paintings. I also spent two years improving my skills in charcoal." For her, the key is being intentional about every detail and carefully choosing colors that capture the spirit of the work. "I concentrate on every single detail. I always use two types of colors: one more 'dreamy' and one more 'realistic.' I use bright, vibrant colors to inspire hope and happiness, and I use darker colors to inspire more reflection on the current reality and its challenges."

Fortuitously, Malak's time at Zarqa University saw many opportunities to showcase her work. She was exposed to a number of international art competitions, and she entered every one of them she could find. Until then, her supporters – her teachers in Damascus and Za'atari, her classmates, her mother and father, Roaa, Hoda, and her eleven other siblings – had complimented her work over and over. But they were probably biased because of their personal relationships with her, she thought, no matter how hard they tried to be objective. Now was a time to see how much her art could affect and inspire strangers.

Malak's first opportunity to test this was a competition held on the other side of the world in the United States. Without high expectations, Malak submitted one of her paintings for consideration. To her joyful surprise, she was selected by the judges for the second-place prize. Though she could not travel to the US to receive her award in person, this and another competition held locally in Za'atari were pivotal turning points for Malak. "All of my family members were very proud, motivating me and cheering me on. My sister Hoda complimented my drawings and gave me good feedback. My dad encouraged me and gave me feedback, too." With all the energy, praise, and attention they brought to her art, these competitions would be the catalyst Malak needed to formally launch her venture. No longer would art take a back seat; as an entrepreneur, Malak would place a greater focus on art while she continued her medical analysis studies.

Realizing Malak needed a digital presence to take advantage of the sudden interest in her work, Roaa and Malak set up Instagram and Facebook pages. Hundreds of followers poured in. Orders started coming in via direct messages, especially from her peers at university and attendees at the international art competitions. Malak would travel to acquire additional supplies as she geared up for the sudden increase in production. She made a point to always go in person herself: "I go to Amman myself because I know the type and quality of the material I want. There is a special type of pencil I like to draw with."

Malak's studio – called simply "Malak Art" – was born.

Malak and Roaa cared deeply about instilling the spirit that had developed at these competitions in their adoptive home, Za'atari. Though Za'atari still did not have much of a market for art, Malak and Roaa wanted to fuel an artistic movement in the camp nonetheless. Malak became a part of a group of local artists called Film Za'atari, which coordinated several galleries in the Za'atari bazaar. Visitors and locals attend the galleries, and Malak made her first in-person sale of a painting to a visitor for $100.

"In the bazaar, you have to be there with your paintings to tell people about them." Never a natural self-promoter, this was not always easy for Malak. This is where Roaa, as always seems to be the case, completed her. "[For a long time] no one in our neighborhood knew that I'm an artist, because I'm always drawing in my tent. I'm shy, so I have often refused interviews. But my sisters are always proud of me and telling everyone about my talent. And Roaa is my manager – she knows everything about me [and shares my work]."

One work that Malak made during this period of great progress stands out to her. It was for an international competition, hosted at Amman's Princess Sumaya University for Technology, that was centered on the theme of human rights. The topic was perfect because it reminded

Malak and Roaa about what they ultimately hoped to accomplish through art: to affect people's lives. They had first met, after all, debating about social issues. Now, the duo could use art to communicate messages that might improve the lives of their neighbors throughout Za'atari, especially the young people of their generation.

For this competition, Malak opted to show off her advanced skills in charcoal. Her charcoal drawing depicted a young girl with eyes widened in shock, her mouth covered by two large and weathered hands. As Malak explains, the darkness cast upon the hands together with the black background represent an oppressive current state, while the brightness in the girl's eyes represents a pure hope for the future. Though the drawing is in black and white, Malak was still able to employ her classic style of balancing "dreamy" and "realistic" emotions. Meant to shine a light on the issue of child marriage in Za'atari and around the world, the drawing is a breathtaking reminder of what is at stake if the practice continues: the lives and well-being of millions of girls.

Malak's drawing won the competition's top prize. The recognition was wonderful, but this piece of art also sparked a mission: Malak desired to share these types of works more widely in Za'atari – to help end the victimization of girls in her adoptive home.

── ∗ ──

This progress in Yasmina's, Malak's, and Asma's ventures became symbolic of and a catalyst for broader change in Za'atari. As people's passions and skills started to shine through during the first few months and years, the camp – now with rows and rows of trailers as far as the eye can see – increasingly showed signs of life.

Perhaps the most symbolic transformation could be seen on the main business road, in many ways the heart of the camp: Market Street. The "Market Street" label was a default one set by camp administration – simply an identifier of the function the road was meant to play in the camp. But as Za'atari residents launched startups on the street and made it their own, Market Street began to slowly transform into something more. The residents nicknamed it the "Shams-Élysées" – a playful fusion of the Champs-Élysées in Paris and the Arabic word for Syria: "al-Sham."[1] People were given trailers for free on the street and were able to use them with fewer restrictions than before. New stores popped up across the Shams-Élysées.

The sparks of a few early entrepreneurs were lighting the way for others. There was a bit more color in Za'atari thanks to Malak and her fellow artists. There were more social events like weddings prepared by Yasmina. And there were more social programs to enrich children's time like Asma's storytelling initiative.

Once a week, Asma would open her wooden front door and call out loudly so that all the neighbors could hear:

"Yalla lil kisa, ya shabaab!" "Come for the story, young ones!"

Over time, emerging from the wooden door for the weekly invitation would not just be Asma. There would be another, smaller figure by her side: Nawara. After Nawara's first drawing stood out to Asma, the two became very close. Nawara took on the role of apprentice. She would follow Asma around, helping her select the books to read and the activities to run with the children. Nawara soon looked up to Asma so much that she would refer to Asma as her "second mom." Asma shares with joy:

"Nawara liked to watch how I worked with the children. She used to say to me, 'I want to be like you, mom.' And now she is reading to the children alongside me."

Thanks to Asma's hours of practice, her imploring of children to join the initiative, and Nawara's trusted assistance, Stories of the Sun was growing. In the past, it had felt like pulling teeth to get kids to take part. Now, the storytelling group had become a well-attended fixture in the children's lives: on certain afternoons each week, it was time to gather at Professor Asma's trailer. Nawara, as a peer of the children in the group, could easily update them should timing change. She was the chief marketer, and the group continued to grow as friends of friends joined and soon became regulars.

Not only was attendance increasing, but progress was clear. The first activity that Asma led with the children, in which nearly all of them drew symbols of war, weighed heavily on her mind. Her role, she felt, was to empower the children to be more optimistic about creating their own futures, more engaged in the community, more self-confident, and, of course, more adept at reading, speaking, writing, and otherwise composing and communicating their ideas. As she implemented new activities with Nawara's support, Asma monitored the children closely.

One activity in particular, held a year into the initiative during the Eid celebration, stands out in Asma's memory as the moment she realized there was real growth – that the hours she spent with the children were succeeding in transforming their thoughts, hopes, and visions for the future. After reading a story, with Nawara's help, Asma gathered together dozens of uninflated colored balloons and markers and passed them out to the children. Then, she asked the students – exactly as she had for that fateful first activity a year before – to write or draw whatever was on their minds. She braced herself for more of the same.

Much to her joy, the outcome was starkly different. "They drew flowers, trees, colorful things." Then came the really fun part: Asma told the kids to inflate their balloons. She opened the wooden door, and instructed them to run outside the trailer and gather together. With the whole group standing outside the trailer in the Za'atari heat, Asma counted down. "Thalatha, Ithnan, Wahid" – "Three, Two, One." All at once, dozens of colorful balloons were released, rising gently into the sky above Za'atari. They were being sent off to Syria, Asma tells the kids.

"The children were very, very happy."

CHAPTER 8

Extreme Entrepreneurs

These are not your classic startups.

Refugees around the world are often as far from the pop-culture image of entrepreneurs as they could possibly get. They usually do not enjoy the benefits of extensive networks, incubators, accelerators, startup competitions, and the promise of jaw-dropping amounts of investment capital if they can strike the right tone in their pitch meetings. Worlds away from the resource-rich Silicon Valley, refugees are frequently living in temporary structures in camps or in low-income communities within cities where they are hosted or resettled.

Refugee entrepreneurs usually come to a new place with next to nothing, and they innovate for their lives. They are the most extreme entrepreneurs on the planet.

These entrepreneurs face greater obstacles than perhaps any other class of entrepreneurs in the world. Beyond the lack of networks and external resources available to them, they usually have little-to-no savings and room for error. And they often have limited preparation for entrepreneurship before being thrown into it; many did not have entrepreneurial jobs back at home, had their education interrupted by the chaos that spurred them to leave, or had not worked before. As we begin a discussion of these challenges encountered by refugees, it is worth noting that many of these obstacles are common among other categories of migrants – including internally displaced persons (IDPs) who are forced to leave their homes but do not cross national borders, and immigrants who choose to leave their countries in pursuit of economic opportunity.

The most obvious of the challenges confronted by refugee entrepreneurs, both in camps and in cities, is money. The issue is two-pronged: First, when it comes to personal savings, refugees frequently have nothing but the clothes on their backs and, as in the case of Yasmina's family, a few bags of belongings thrown together in haste. Second, it is usually very difficult to find capital in any form – due to refugees' lack of established credit histories, language and technology barriers, and discriminatory practices by financial institutions. And even capital alone is insufficient; refugee entrepreneurs rightfully worry about ensuring they are receiving trusted money. In the complicated world of small-business loans and investments, there is little guidance on what a reasonable interest rate is, what institutions are predatory, and what kinds of investments are one-sided. In camps and temporary host cities, there is sometimes an added complication: entrepreneurship can be illegal for refugees. This leads them to start informal businesses, which means they are not able to benefit from governmental resources that can be quite valuable, especially in early stages when entrepreneurs lack other sources of capital.[1]

Then comes the dearth of personal and familial networks. Just as they often arrive at new places without savings, refugees come with limited – or virtually zero – personal or professional networks. As a result, they do not have readily accessible advising or mentorship related to their businesses, from the decision point of whether to take the plunge in the first place to the tactics of scaling a business over time. Beyond specific business-related advising, refugee entrepreneurs often do not have anyone with relative power locally to help navigate operational issues. With such a lack of personal support, even a bit of encouragement from local community members and institutions can make all the difference. Consider the words of Balighah, a Yemeni refugee working as part of a refugee-led artisan collaborative hosted by a refugee resettlement organization in the Rust Belt town of Utica, New York:

> I was told when I first came here that as a single mom and refugee, I would not make it. That I should just go back home [to Yemen]. Advising and encouragement [from the local refugee center] meant a lot to me to overcome that.[2]

Discrimination is another obstacle, especially in today's increasingly politicized climate around the topic of immigration. There are meaningful barriers to mutual understanding and acceptance of refugees and of migrants more broadly. To succeed, refugee entrepreneurs need some level of community buy-in and support, so any entrenchment of negative opinions about them because of where they came from, or how they got there, hinders their potential success. Unfortunately, migrants are often portrayed in the media as merely "victims" (i.e., charity cases meant only to be pitied, without their own powerful voices and abilities) or as "villains" (i.e., criminals wreaking havoc on their new communities) – either way, as one-dimensional and not as fully equal human beings. As an example of the villainization element, a study featured in *Forbes* has shown that Black, Latino, and Middle Eastern immigrant characters in the US media are depicted as criminals at a startlingly high frequency.[3] These dehumanizing and inaccurate media portrayals erect barriers to treating refugees and immigrants with the dignity they deserve – and thus to welcoming and investing in them appropriately.

Adding to all of these difficulties, as we saw in Za'atari, are significant mental health challenges. The grind of entrepreneurship – the risk-taking, the ups and downs, the uncertainty and self-doubt, the desire to quit, the balancing of personal and family commitments – already weigh heavily. But having to go through those trials and challenges amidst the type of loss, grief, emotional anguish, and mental limbo faced by refugees is not easy to fathom.

Dealing with a difficult customer is harder when, like Yasmina, you receive calls from your family members updating you about the ongoing war in your hometown. Tweaking a marketing strategy is tougher when, like Malak, you were torn from your home as a teenager and have had to come to grips with an upbringing that was once the stuff of your worst nightmares. And performing well each day is more challenging when, like Asma, you have a hole in your heart from the loss of a child.

※ ——— ※ ——— ※

So how could a refugee entrepreneurship phenomenon emerge, despite all the odds against it?

Even with the overwhelming challenges refugees face compared to the average aspiring entrepreneur, they outpace native-born citizens in starting businesses. In the US, for example, 9 percent of native-born Americans are entrepreneurs, compared to 13 percent of refugees.[4] The same pattern holds in other nations; in Australia, refugees are nearly twice as likely as native-born individuals to be entrepreneurs.[5] Meanwhile, refugees have created entrepreneurial ecosystems from scratch in camps all over the world. Ultimately, refugees' innovative sparks are notably more common than those of other individuals, and the same holds true for migrants more generally.

These sparks are not ignited by accident. Though the experience is far from uniform, refugees tend to have several common qualities stemming from the shared experience of being forced to flee home that make them more likely to come up with – and see through – compelling startup ideas. So many of the classic qualities that are celebrated in entrepreneurs – so many of the characteristics investors look for in founders, so many of the qualities entrepreneurs write about in their how-to books, so many of the motivational lessons with thousands of likes on

LinkedIn feeds – are found within refugees. The rest of this chapter explores five of these qualities.

The first and most obvious reason for the refugee entrepreneurship phenomenon connects to the sobering circumstances faced by refugees: for many, innovation is the only means to survive. *Needing* to innovate is markedly different than simply *wanting* to or *preferring* to; innovation is many refugees' one shot at a stable livelihood. This fact spurs them to give all they have to their ventures, as they know those ventures might be their only hope for their families' survival and well-being. As one advocate for investment in refugee-founded ventures explained it: "They are the quintessential extreme entrepreneurs. They have gone through hell, endured it, and now are rebuilding their lives. There is maybe a bigger commitment because this is their best chance at hope."[6]

So, through these dire circumstances, a common quality emerges among refugees: an ability to boldly take risks in starting and operating new ventures, and a penchant for going all in.

Take Za'atari, for example. Unlike many of their counterparts around the world, the entrepreneurs in Za'atari are mostly not starting businesses only for the thrill of it, or because they desire wealth and fame, or because their old jobs were too stuffy. For Za'atari's entrepreneurs, their businesses are frequently their lifelines. This is the case for Yasmina; for her, innovating is not a hobby, but a requirement to provide for her children. Yes, the passion for hairdressing and wedding preparation flows through Yasmina's veins, but the decision to launch her shop in

Za'atari was almost entirely about her kids. She would have much rather held off on selling her jewelry and waited for a return to Syria, but holding off would mean her children might not have enough to eat. Starting her salon was a risk that she knew she had to take for her family, and thus one she did not have time to second-guess as entrepreneurs with a comfortable "next best alternative" might. Yasmina had to be fully committed from day one.

Or consider a story highlighted by the UNHCR and the Norwegian Refugee Council about a woman named Masika, an entrepreneur in the Sherkole camp in Ethiopia. A few thousand miles south of the scorching Za'atari sun in Jordan, across the Red Sea and down the mighty Nile, near the border between Ethiopia and Sudan, is Sherkole. The dry desert air is replaced with suffocating humidity, the sand with lush green, the vertical grain with hanging mango trees, the plains with rolling hills, and the metal trailers with clay huts. Unlike Za'atari, which is made up entirely of Syrians, Sherkole's residents hail from a range of countries in Africa, fleeing myriad life-threatening circumstances – a unique community fabric woven together by drought, war, and genocide. And more than twice as old as Za'atari, Sherkole has existed now for over twenty years, with a generation having grown into adulthood knowing no life but camp life.[7]

Masika was a taxi driver back in the Democratic Republic of the Congo's lively capital city of Kinshasa, returning home each night to her loving husband and children. But she was forced to flee what is sometimes referred to as "Africa's first world war" in Congo after a series of brutal assaults on her family: her husband was killed, her daughter was abused and raped by soldiers fighting in the war, and her son was kidnapped. Shell-shocked, she, her mother, her five children, and her grandson found their way to Sherkole.[8]

As was the case for Yasmina, entrepreneurship was the only path forward for Masika to support her family – and she gave it all she had. She shared with the UNCHR: "[W]hen I arrived in Sherkole, I didn't have a lot of money for me and my kids. I looked for jobs, applied for jobs[,] but I felt no one could help me."[9]

Determined, Masika was able to secure $72 in seed funding from the Norwegian Refugee Council to start a restaurant and bakery.[10] Her venture struggled early on, but a major breakthrough eventually came: a contract to cater for the camp's International Women's Day event. Masika was a hit at the gathering, and her startup, finally, began to take off. With more successful catering contracts as catalysts, she reached significant scale to the point of baking 1,500 loaves of bread a day. And with a bit more funding, she expanded the business and brought in three partners.[11]

Masika's entrepreneurship was fueled by the fight to keep her kids alive; she was as all-in on her startup as it gets. This was even more the case as the number of kids she had to provide for grew, suddenly, from five to eight; Masika brought into her already jam-packed home three orphan boys who were alone in Sherkole. "If you are under my roof, then you are family whether I gave birth to you or not."[12] Masika is thankful she could bring them in and, through her new entrepreneurial life in Sherkole, support them after everything they had endured:

> It brings tears to my eyes when I look at them sometimes, but I am glad I took them in. They go to school and they have a place to call home[,] and a family that loves and takes care of them.[13]

�֍——✳——✵

A second reason refugees are more likely to be entrepreneurs is that they enjoy the benefit of exposure to other cultures, working styles, and markets. This is a competitive advantage that enables them to think outside of existing structures in a way other individuals might not.

As a study published in the *Harvard Business Review* demonstrated, cross-cultural experiences give people an edge in entrepreneurship because their experiences expose them to other customer preferences, types of products and services, and ways of thinking and doing business. Using undergraduate students to test their hypothesis, researchers found that students who lived and studied abroad for a semester generated significantly stronger business ideas upon their return than they had before their cultural exchange. The control group, students who stayed at their home university, actually generated slightly worse business ideas at the end of the semester than they had at the beginning of it. In a separate experiment focused on a group of migrant entrepreneurs living in Austria, researchers found that activating memories of their past cross-cultural experiences helped them create better startup ideas.[14]

Malak is an example of this cross-cultural experience advantage at work. Aside from Malak's brilliant talents, one appeal of her art is the ability to infuse a Syrian flair. Many of her online customers demonstrate a desire to explore and understand a culture they were previously unfamiliar with. So, when entrepreneurs like Malak introduce products connected to their home country into a foreign marketplace, they are both expanding the array of offerings and satisfying customers in a way that traditional offerings cannot. It is part of the reason several Syrian pastry shops in Za'atari do so well among customers in Jordanian cities outside the camp, who place catering orders for major gatherings. Moreover, beyond these benefits to customers, this type of intercultural exchange carries with it the invaluable byproduct of creating greater mutual understanding and appreciation across differences.

The cross-cultural experience advantage can also be seen in refugee-welcoming cities around the world, where refugees are introducing new business models and products. Often, what may seem impossible to locals is simple and straightforward to refugees. Refugees can see opportunities where others cannot.

Take Razan. She fled Damascus in 2012 after an explosion at her husband's office made clear they had to leave to protect their children's lives. She and her family sought asylum in Yorkshire, England. With two degrees in tow, and the ability to speak four languages, Razan was immensely qualified – but she could not find work in her new home.

Her description to an interviewer in the UK of the pain and disappointment of not being able to get a job, after striving to build up her credentials back at home, is poignant:

> When things got bad in Syria, I thought my qualifications would secure me a decent job if I had to leave. But when you just wait in the job centre with no offers, it feels like being stabbed in the heart.[15]

But unsurprisingly, given what she had gone through, Razan did not give up. She started from scratch, thought back to her passions and background in Damascus, and came up with an idea people born and raised in Yorkshire might be unlikely to develop:

> I started to think, "What am I good [at]?" I'm kind of a foodie person. I love cooking, and I love cheese actually. And I noticed that halloumi cheese is not available all seasons in the UK.[16]

Halloumi cheese is popular in Syria. Razan noticed that the resources in her new home that could be used to make halloumi cheese were being underutilized:

> The milk here is really great. Maybe the local people cannot feel that because they gr[e]w up with it. But coming from the Middle East, I noticed how wonderful ... the milk [is]. And I started to think: what if I make halloumi cheese out of British milk?[17]

Through the help of a government program, she received training and mentorship and secured a £2,500 loan to buy the initial materials she needed. And she never looked back. Now her venture – Yorkshire Dama Cheese (Dama is short for Damascus) – is a fan favorite, with annual revenues of more than £100,000, broad distribution, and a gold medal at the World Cheese Awards.[18] An award-winning business-woman with eight employees depending on her, Razan – like many refugee entrepreneurs around the world – was able to notice the beauty in her adoptive home in a way that others could not. And she was able to fuse that local knowledge with what she learned from her intercultural experiences to create breakthrough opportunities in the town that wel-comed her. Razan's husband said it well: "With Yorkshire milk and Syrian know-how, we will make the UK the hal-loumi capital of the world."[19]

—❋—

A fundamental quality of entrepreneurship is the ability to empathize with the needs of one's customers and to be fervently driven to serve those needs. Therein lies a third reason refugees stand out as entrepreneurs: because of their past struggles and their desire to create new communities where they land, refugees are often intensely motivated to find ways to serve the needs of those in their second homes. Their ventures are frequently marked by a passionate focus on helping others – a refreshing perspective in a world of entrepreneurship that can be much too self-oriented, and all the more admirable given that refugees have so many press-ing needs of their own.

In refugee camps, the residents living together have gone through similarly traumatic experiences. Many rode together in caravans or sailed together in makeshift boats to flee their homes. This leads to a profound sense of community – bonded by shared trials and driven by shared optimism, even through the toughest of times. Because of their resultant ability to empathize with their potential customers' experiences, refugees can design services and products that meet their communities' needs and desires at the deepest levels.

Asma is an example. Her spark stemmed from an overwhelming aspiration to support and empower her new community – an aspiration intensified by the loss of her child. She manifested this through a custom-designed social initiative that serves the most pressing needs of children in Za'atari. A similar example, in the Budubaram camp in Ghana, is Karrus. A refugee from Liberia, Karrus was forced to flee for his life and leave his family behind. He was alone in Budubaram – a camp of Liberians who, like him, had fled the country's civil wars – and was saddened to see the children around him with no free schooling options.[20] With a $50 loan and space donated by a church in the camp, he launched a school that has since developed into its own building and a broader nonprofit educating students both in Ghana and back home in Liberia, where there has been peace since 2003.[21] Though he had no family around him or children of his own, he was naturally able to empathize with the parents in the camp because of their shared struggle: "When you look at these children, you see abilities, you see aspirations. The future of the nation depends on them. Without the chance to study, an entire generation will be at risk."[22]

In cities, too, refugees' understanding of what it means to lack community and to have lost everything often fuels a burning desire to find ways to serve those in their adoptive homes. This is frequently their way of connecting and making a new place begin to feel like home. The software entrepreneur Dame Stephanie "Steve" Shirley originally arrived in the UK after fleeing Nazi Germany as a Jewish child refugee – a five-year-old alone with her nine-year-old sister. Throughout her life in England, she has been entrepreneurial not just in launching her company but also in donating most of her wealth to innovative public causes.[23] Steve has connected her refugee story to why she strives to serve those around her: "I do it because of my personal history; I need to justify the fact that my life was saved."[24] A refugee from Somaliland, Muna was just a few years older than Steve was when she arrived in the UK, accompanied by her mother and little brother. She went on to launch a home care agency that now employs seventy people. Partly because she was bullied as a teenager due to where she came from, she now actively seeks to "break down social barriers between her largely Somali workforce and her mostly white clients."[25] As she put it: "I'm doing my bit for integration."[26] Both Steve and Muna demonstrate an empathy for their new neighbors, born from a gratitude to be alive and a desire to build a supportive community to call "home."

Finally, consider Chip, a web developer in Utica. Chip spent part of her childhood in a refugee camp in southern Thailand, and she has just one photograph to remember her time there. It is a grainy image of a young Chip, with a bowl cut, eating ice cream with her two sisters and smiling from ear to ear. A childlike joy amidst the hardest times.

Chip was born in Laos, a mountainous Southeast Asian country bordering Vietnam (expecting that you haven't heard of Laos, she always has that quick tagline on the tip of her tongue). A few months after the Vietnam War, she and her siblings were woken up suddenly in the middle of the night; they were to board a small boat crossing the Mekong River, manned by teenagers, to flee for safety.

That was the last time she would be in Laos, and her time in Thailand would be fleeting. Her family would be split apart, and she and her mother would be resettled to America, fatefully directed to upstate New York. The refugee camp in Thailand behind her, she would negotiate a new identity: that of a refugee woman in America. There would be self-doubt, struggle, and insecurity attached to that label.

But several members of the Utica community would support and uplift her. First among them would be a local pastor. After Chip and her mom arrived in the dead of winter wearing flip-flops and shorts, the pastor allowed them to live in his congregation's steeple until they could afford an apartment. Later down the road, Chip's support would come from a college professor and mentor who believed in her even when she didn't fully believe in herself. After working at an app development company for a few years in nearby Syracuse, Chip made a brave decision: to take a leap of faith and start her own app development startup, CNY Apps (CNY stands for Central New York).

Now, she looks back at her grainy picture from Thailand with a warm smile. Chip, the refugee girl from a place most people around her had never heard of, would become for many the heartbeat of an old factory town in blue-collar America – the town that welcomed her. Her company is helping local small businesses leverage technology to better reach and serve customers. From her trendy office in downtown Utica, Chip is now in the midst of expanding her app development services internationally and launching two other startups with her husband. Through both her entrepreneurship and her community leadership, she is an active contributor to Utica's revitalization and a beloved part of the stories of so many Utican families. "I'm finally living the dream," she says cheerfully. Importantly, for Chip living the dream means more than independence, the thrill of entrepreneurship, or money; it means serving and empowering the community that had supported her when she and her family had no one to rely on.[27]

∗——∗——∗

A fourth reason for refugees' heightened entrepreneurship is employment discrimination. Due to discrimination in the workplace as well as in education, refugees are often driven away from traditional employment and into new ventures where they are more in control of their own fates.

Many times, this type of discrimination is subtle. A recent study found that African American and Asian American job applicants in the US who "whitened" their resumes (for example, by removing references to their ethnic affinity groups) received more interviews.[28] Studies continue to reveal hiring discrimination against applicants with "ethnic-sounding" names – including names perceived as Arab,[29] Latino, and Black.[30] Driven by a combination of implicit and intentional bias, this employment discrimination can "exert pressure on [migrants] to seek self-employment."[31] Employers and professional associations can also discriminate against refugees by refusing to recognize foreign qualifications and training[32] – a phenomenon known as "brain waste."[33] Rather than accepting a position for which they are significantly overqualified (called by some "mal-employment," a form of underemployment), many refugees choose instead to launch their own businesses.[34]

The examples of discrimination are countless, and their links to entrepreneurship are common. Muna experienced discrimination from an early age at school before it helped strengthen her path in entrepreneurship: "I hated it. I didn't want to be a refugee. At first, I just wanted to go back to my country."[35] Balighah, along with so many others, was underestimated and counted out; entrepreneurship, in partnership with the artisan collaborative that respected her clothing design talents, was her way forward as well.

Finally, underlying all of these reasons that refugees tend to excel as entrepreneurs are two complementary qualities: resilience, and the ability to continually find dignity and joy in being an entrepreneur.

Refugees' innovative tendencies are just another beautiful example of their resilience. Even after seeing their family members killed in front of them, or having their houses burned to the ground, or facing violent assaults and threats to their lives, these individuals push on. Rather than give in to the forces around them, they leave home and then piece their families' lives back together in a foreign place. Muna explained how this resilience makes for steelier entrepreneurship: "You become more resilient, which you need to be as an entrepreneur. The struggles and the hardship you go through make you stronger than other people."[36]

Fueling some of this resilience, too, is a deep appreciation for the dignity in entrepreneurship. When refugees are limited in other opportunities, as many are, innovation becomes the only chance to feel the sense of agency employment can provide. As Masika put it, "I am now a self-sufficient woman. And I am proud of it."[37] Or, as Ismail – a Syrian coffee shop owner in the Ritsona camp in Greece – said, "This coffee shop brings forth humanity and ethics . . . . Work is the jewel of man. I cannot sit at home."[38]

An accompanying sense of joy often pervades refugee entrepreneurs' work, making it easier to get through difficult stretches. To truly enjoy entrepreneurship, it might be that it should always feel like a privilege and not something we are entitled to; refugee entrepreneurs know this better than anyone. For many entrepreneurs, innovating becomes a chore; though it may start as a passionate activity of imagining a new world around them and going out and creating it, it loses its sparkle over time. While refugee entrepreneurs are of course prone to the same frustrations, there is joy underlying their work. Joy bred from knowing that at one point when they left home they had nothing, and now they get to rebuild a life on their own terms, based on their own ideas.

Joy of a life restored by entrepreneurship.

Razan summarized her joy with a bursting smile: "I fled the war in Syria to secure my family's future and now I'm running an award-winning cheese business in Yorkshire. And I couldn't be happier than that."[39]

Part III

Revival

> *To be called a refugee is the opposite of an insult;*
> *it is a badge of strength, courage, and victory.*
> —Tennessee Office for Refugees

CHAPTER 9

Midnight Blue

Thanks in part to Malak, Za'atari has been infused with art and color.

The once-drab, gray walls on the edges of the camp are painted with murals; Malak and dozens of children decorated one of these walls in celebration of World Refugee Day. Among the most beautiful and prominent of the paintings is of a woman with her hand out in a gesture of acceptance. Her hijab is colored in dazzling interconnected diamonds of purple, green, and white. It is a vibrant symbol of love and care for others. And it is far from what one might imagine if asked to describe the entrance to a refugee camp.

This is just one of the many ways that Za'atari entrepreneurs have transformed life in the camp, both from an economic and a social perspective. While the camp is certainly still insufficient in terms of resources to support its residents, the impact residents have had on improving life for themselves and their neighbors is nothing short of incredible. The type of heroic work that deserves the world's attention.

A far cry from its makeshift origins, Za'atari is now in many ways like a city. The Shams-Élysées, Saudi Market, and other areas are buzzing as more than 3,000 businesses generate about $13 million in revenue a month and grow to serve community members' needs.[1] The ventures launched by Yasmina, Asma, and Malak are emblematic of a spirit of innovation that has captivated the camp. Za'atari's rate of entrepreneurship today is estimated at 12.5 percent, meaning more than one of every ten residents is an entrepreneur.[2] For comparison, this is almost triple the rate of native-born entrepreneurs in the rest of Jordan.[3]

In place of a barren sand pathway arose a bustling street of startups. In place of occasional secondhand clothing stores and isolated sales of basic products from home trailers arose a clothing emporium, bike shops, restaurants, arcades, supermarkets, barbershops, and cell phone retailers. In place of spending time alone at home emerged a vibrant singing competition, murals by the Za'atari Art Committee, and a taekwondo championship for girls like Tamara and Maya. And in place of the fruitless desert arose green energy in the form of the largest solar plant ever built in a refugee camp and sustainable farming efforts pioneered by Za'atari residents.[4]

A walk down the Shams-Élysées or Saudi Market around midday tells a story of vibrance and creativity. Za'atari residents clothe mannequins in front of their stores. Birds chirp loudly from the occasional bird shops, especially meaningful in Za'atari as birds are considered by many residents a symbol of freedom. Horses carry carts of produce and Coca-Cola bottles to grocery stores, and pizzas emerge from fiery clay ovens. Classic Syrian pastries – with perfectly baked proportions of phyllo dough, pistachios, dates, syrup, powdered sugar, and more – are handled on huge silver pans. Bikes whiz by, their riders ringing bells to alert those moving too slowly in front of them. Occasionally, a yellow bus will come by and children, with their oversized backpacks, will step out to join the commotion and skip along.

And, inevitably if you are in Saudi Market, the colorful Salon of Lights will stop you in your tracks. Today, Yasmina continues, strong as ever, with her full-service bridal preparation business. Her work is seasonal, and during the busiest of wedding periods she is working nonstop with several clients at a time. Yasmina also demonstrates daily that the entrepreneurship movement in Za'atari goes far deeper than revenue and economic growth. She is bringing profound joy to the lives of women across Za'atari. She helps brides feel special, accepted, valued, and beautiful, sometimes after a long period of feeling forgotten.

Building on that legacy of impact, Asma's storytelling initiative has grown dramatically since its early days – with eager students regularly filling her trailer. More than a weekly experience, the storytelling group is a bedrock community for many of Za'atari's children. So much so that even during celebrations and occasions in the camp, kids often come to Asma's peaceful trailer to listen to stories rather than attend the bigger events.

Moreover, Asma's operations have expanded into a multipronged social initiative. She organizes her children to drive civic engagement efforts, like picking up trash in the camp. She regularly issues calls to action to children and adults alike through her role as a writer in the local newspaper; just one example is her op-ed aimed at mobilizing community members to plant trees throughout the camp. And she publishes her poetry in a Za'atari magazine, another channel through which she uplifts her neighbors.

The children in Za'atari, in turn, are starting to innovate at a young age. As aid organizations have seen the incredible organic growth of Za'atari ventures, they have leaned in to support ideas taking shape in the minds of residents – including youths. And they rely on local teachers much like Asma to lead the way. A Tufts University-sponsored STEM (Science, Technology, Engineering, and Math) project called Design Squad Club is an example.[5] The program, operated by Za'atari teachers, tasks children with identifying problems in the camp community, and then devising technology-based solutions to address them.[6] The solutions the children have designed thus far – a hydroponic garden, for instance – are aimed at improving the quality of life in Za'atari.[7] As the Design Squad Club project lead sees it, "We are empowering the next generation. These are the future engineers who will go back to rebuild their cities."[8]

Meanwhile, several organizations host programs helping those who otherwise lack opportunities to cultivate their talents. Fatima, a woman who lost her hearing as a child due to a medical error, found a home in one such initiative: a women's center led by the Institute of Family Health and the UN Population Fund.[9] The program includes dedicated services for women and girls, like counseling and communication of important health information. Early on, Fatima was discouraged by having to find a new community in Za'atari and again face the disability stigma she endured growing up: "At first, I was really frustrated by the reaction of the people and their way of treating me [because] I'm with special needs."[10] But she became a volunteer in the program, using her artistic abilities to teach sewing and painting classes and earning a stipend for her service. Fatima recounted, "The ... women's [center] discovered and believed in my talents and encouraged me to improve those skills .... I got a new, great opportunity to be happy again."[11]

Art in Za'atari inevitably brings us back to Malak. The studio has been going quite well. It has been going so well, in fact, that she has had to refuse online orders so that she can focus on her studies and clinical training.[12] From her childhood, Malak knew that she wanted to use art to help people; money was never the primary motivator. The international human rights competition for which she crafted the charcoal drawing on the topic of child marriage re-sparked in her a desire to use her skills to support her younger peers more directly.

Malak's role as a volunteer at a youth center in Za'atari presented the perfect opportunity. The center was planning to hold a series of sessions to raise awareness about the harms of child marriage.[13] One practice that has been shown to successfully combat child marriage is "empowering girls with information, skills, and support networks" – in addition to mobilizing parents and community members, providing crucial economic support for girls and their families, and more.[14] So the youth center aimed to do its part by communicating as clearly as possible to the girls of Za'atari the risks of child marriage, and giving them the sense of purpose and confidence to push back on such arrangements.

Malak jumped at the opportunity to contribute. Back at her trailer, sitting on the ground with her midnight blue colored pencil, Malak worked into the nights to finish her drawings ahead of the youth forum. She designed a series of twenty powerful, comic-style sketches – meant to instill confidence, while powerfully expressing that child marriage exposes girls to abuse and prevents them from reaching their full potential. It was a difficult balance.

Thankfully, the event ended up being more of a success than Malak could have imagined. Near the final moments of a workshop that included speakers and group discussions, she presented the drawings to the girls. They observed the artwork silently, and then discussed in small groups what each drawing meant to them.

Back at the plenary session, the girls were asked to summarize the day. Malak was moved by the response: "At the end, several girls stood up to announce that they were ending their marital engagements and returning to school."

"Art is my way of communicating with others. People often don't like you to advise them directly, but you can get to them through art. In the drawings, you can see questions and the answers to those questions. Many people, children and parents, took in the advice through the drawings – and it really changed their minds."

CHAPTER 10

Dignity

Jordanian pop music blasts throughout the studio. A sleek-haired man in a navy blazer opens the side door. Out comes Malak.

All while the music plays on, the man directs her to the moon-shaped desk and pulls out a fancy white chair for her. Malak sits down. He adjusts the microphone in front of her, and gestures to explain the basics: lean forward when you speak, lean backwards when you're listening. The music is still blaring as Malak puts on the big black headphones covering her ears, brings out her phone to turn it off, and looks forward to face the microphone. Her eyes wide and her eyebrows raised in a seeming combination of anxiety and amusement.

This is the studio of 106.5 FM "The Meeting." Painted across the back wall is a mural of the red buildings of the ancient city of Petra, the most visited site in Jordan. In front of the mural, anchoring the moon-shaped desk, are two young Jordanians: Maha and Mohamed, the hosts of "Shabaabjee" ("Youth"), a radio show for Jordanian youth.

Mohamed in a long-sleeved white shirt with thin black stripes, sporting a trimly cut beard. Maha in a pink dress, matching hijab, and focused expression. Each wearing big black headphones to match Malak. In the back corner of the room is a Jordanian flag, with its red chevron and black, white, and green horizontal stripes.

Moments earlier, Mohamed, with his energetic voice speaking in swift Arabic, had introduced today's special show. It was to be about young entrepreneurs, he explained, to help them come up with and see their ideas through – ideas that could be impactful to their communities. Mohamed delivered the prompts for the show: "How can we start small projects to advance us forward? How can we face challenges and competition? How can we create a fresh start to improve our lives?" The two hosts began by taking a handful of questions from aspiring entrepreneurs watching on Facebook Live, and gave brief advice on designing and launching business ideas. Then the hosts ushered in a commercial break, cuing the blaring theme music.

Shortly after Malak's entrance, the music stops suddenly. After some banter with Maha, Mohamed shifts attention quickly:

MOHAMED: "Let us welcome our first guest, Malak, the artist. She is going to share with us her experiences, her paintings, her competitions. To tell you the truth, her paintings are incredible. The type of paintings that people can stand in front of and stare at for five minutes."

MAHA:	"Ahlan wa sahlan." "Welcome."
MALAK:	"Ahlan wa sahlan bi kum." "Welcome to you." [A common response in Arabic.]
MAHA:	"For everyone listening who doesn't know Malak, tell us about yourself."
MALAK:	"My name is Malak and I'm twenty-three years old. I study medical analysis. I live in the Za'atari camp and have been in Jordan for six years."

This radio appearance was not in her comfort zone. It was not even in the zone next to her comfort zone. This was the type of thing she would leave to Roaa, or to her dad, or to Hoda. Malak's comfort zone was back at her canvas in her trailer, where she incubated and developed these ideas that have garnered so much love. But she felt a sense of purpose in representing Za'atari.

MOHAMED:	"Was there ever a time when you said, 'I'm going to put art aside because I have to focus on other things?'"
MALAK:	"I felt that before my last year of high school. I felt that this gift would not take me anywhere [in life]. I never expected this – that a lot of people would like my art."
MOHAMED:	"You never expected to get to this level?"
MALAK:	"No, never."

As a student at a university in Jordan, Malak knows the stereotypes surrounding refugee camps all too well. Her peers sometimes ask questions that presuppose Za'atari's residents are helpless, weak individuals – merely victims. As she puts it, "I hate when people think that we always need help. They are very surprised when they learn that we are well-educated and we have talents." Not that she can totally blame them. She herself once feared life in the camp. But while the camp itself still needs significant improvements to adequately support its residents, those residents themselves are nothing short of remarkable. And to Malak, nothing short of family.

Now, thanks to Malak stepping out of her comfort zone to speak as a representative of Za'atari, many more youth in Jordan – including the ones listening to "Shabaabjee" on 106.5 FM – have gotten to know the people in the camp more holistically. And those listeners got to hear some useful entrepreneurial advice from one of the most courageous entrepreneurs they might ever be introduced to. Laughing softly, Malak leaves her audience with a word of wisdom:

MAHA: "Is there any advice you'd like to share with people?"

MALAK: "My advice is that if you have a gift, take advantage of it when you're little. Don't be like me [and delay]. Use it when you're young!"[1]

⁜——※——⁜

Rows and rows and rows of children sit cross-legged in the sand, all facing the same direction, patiently waiting. Together they form a massive semicircle outside of a small but colorfully decorated trailer.

There in the front stands a short figure in an indigo dress. She looks out into the crowd of children, almost like a little prophet about to reveal the future. She welcomes the group, reaches down to pick up a yellow storybook, sits down with them, and begins.

This was vintage storytelling in Za'atari, and, this time, it was not Asma running the show. It was Nawara.

In many ways, the apprentice has matched the master. Nawara – after a couple of years of being Asma's number two – has implemented her own version of the storytelling initiative. Her sessions consistently draw a large number of children. Asma prefers it this way. "Nawara is so intelligent and now she is better than me – her 'mom,'" she says with a bright smile.

Asma especially loves the surprising effect Nawara has on people. Nawara is only twelve years old and still very small in stature. When others think she is too young and write her off, she shines with confidence. Unlike a younger Asma, and thanks to an older Asma's encouragement, Nawara is nothing short of brave in so many of her inter-actions. Asma remembers an example:

"I was asked to train a group of [older] girls [to become storytellers]. Nawara was sitting with them. They were very surprised when they saw her – a very little girl among them. I gave them books to read [aloud], and Nawara performed the best out of all of them. She read the story so well, with hand motions and everything. I'm so proud of her; she is a brave and strong person."

To Asma, Nawara is a symbol of the power of entrepreneurship. Asma chased children around and reached out to parents in the camp to convince them of the value of her storytelling program so that Nawara would not have to. Asma learned how to be confident and lead activities with conviction so that Nawara could see her example, and see herself in that example.

Like Malak, Asma wishes she had started her teaching and storytelling a little earlier in life. She thinks back to her childhood in Dara'a when she would sleep in her school uniform. Now, Nawara is living out the dream Asma had years ago back in Syria, and is a miniature version of what Asma is just now getting to become. Thanks to Asma's trailblazing leadership, new opportunities exist for Nawara and her peers in the Za'atari refugee camp. Asma is driven to continue creating those opportunities.

"My wish is for all girls to finish their education, and to do what they aspire to do. And I hope they will live a better life than we've lived. I hope there will not be any war when they get to my age."

※———※———※

The sand shifts to the quickening beat of the darbuka. Another wedding in Za'atari. But this time, Yasmina would not sit quietly in her salon drinking tea. This time, it was a family celebration. It was Mona's time to be the client – Yasmina's favorite client in the Salon of Lights's history.

Mona's wedding was bittersweet for Yasmina. Bitter because it meant Mona would no longer be working for her; she would be swept off into a new life. Sweet because Mona had become like a daughter to Yasmina, and seeing Mona celebrate in the way that so many other clients had celebrated meant the world to her. Yasmina had witnessed Mona grow up at the salon over their years together – from that first day when she appeared at Yasmina's doorstep meekly asking for a part-time job, to becoming a courageous partner in crime, to dealing with difficult clients, to making the move to Saudi Market, and everything in between.

Yasmina's leadership style – that of a caring, wise boss who gives space to her employees to grow into their true personalities – would continue to shape and uplift the next generation beyond Mona's departure. Today, Yasmina has two new staff members, each of whom have had their fair share of challenges and who deeply appreciate the mentorship and training she provides.

"I have two assistants. One is a twenty-seven-year-old woman – she's a widow and has a son – and the other is a twenty-year-old woman. The two of them help me with washing, drying, straightening, and dyeing brides' hair, and applying brides' makeup."

Even with the new team members, Mona will always occupy a special place in Yasmina's heart. Of all the wonderful things that have come from her venture – critical income for her family, working with and empowering clients, and continuing to do what she has loved to do since she was a kid – her relationship with Mona has been perhaps the most beautiful to her.

Asked if she still talks with Mona now that she no longer works at the Salon of Lights, Yasmina is taken aback and raises her eyebrows. "Tabaen" – "Of course," she says with a side smile. But the relationship is different now, she says . . . obviously, Mona no longer calls Yasmina "boss."

"Now she only calls me 'mom.'"

※———※———※

The startups created by Malak, Asma, and Yasmina are examples of the deeper significance of entrepreneurship in the camp: even more than economic and social impact, entrepreneurship in Za'atari has brought *dignity*.

First, there is the entrepreneurs' work of utilizing their ventures to help others recognize their dignity. This has meant treating their startups as vessels to empower others, both those on their teams and those they serve. Yasmina did this for her apprentice Mona, and Asma did this for her apprentice Nawara. The two duos then amplified this spirit of empowerment and shared it with hundreds of women, children, and families across Za'atari through their ventures. Za'atari residents witnessed this generosity, and they watched as young entrepreneurs like Malak used their talents not just for themselves but to support their peers. Slowly but surely, Za'atari began to feel more like home to many, or at least as much like home as it could.

Second, there is the work of guarding a sense of dignity for Za'atari itself. The entrepreneurs are well aware of the curiosity that outsiders harbor about life within the camp's walls. "Many people wonder what it is like in the camp," as Malak says. The trio is also aware that outsiders often look down on Za'atari residents or see them with only a sense of sympathy, without respecting their equal dignity. Malak's radio show appearance, and her and Roaa's conversations in the halls at Zarqa University, have defended Za'atari as being a community of people like any other. People with families, aspirations, and needs. As Yasmina says when she travels out into Jordanian cities to support weddings there, "This is a city like any place else." The three entrepreneurs help make sure that Za'atari is seen for what it truly is: a place filled with incredible, profoundly equal human beings who love, celebrate, create art, read stories, and do everything else you might imagine in an "ordinary" city. Certainly, there are more severe needs in the camp than in other places, but this takes nothing away from the *people* of Za'atari – and those people are themselves rising to meet the camp's needs with valor.

Third, there is the more personal sense of dignity: for each of the three women, entrepreneurship has been a reminder of her abilities and potential. For Yasmina, the Salon of Lights has harkened back to her dynamic leadership in Dara'a, allowing her to again occupy her natural role of organizer and manager. For Malak, the Malak Art studio has empowered her to embrace, hone, and share her skills in a way that makes a significant difference in people's lives.

But for no one has this reminder of her own personal dignity been more salient than Asma. Take October 11th: the UN's International Day of the Girl. Asma, much to her surprise, delight, and dread all at the same time, was invited to speak at the prime celebratory event in Za'atari. She would be slated to speak last, after a few celebrities and global human rights leaders. Never in a million years would

Asma think she would be asked to be at the center stage of such a festivity.

Asma said yes to the invitation. As she prepared, she felt a confidence and an underlying thrill she had never experienced before. For Asma, being a social entrepreneur meant reviving a dream she had almost let go of back in Syria. In her early days in Za'atari, she dealt with the most tragic moment of her life – and she thought she would never feel like herself again. Now, Asma feels more personally emboldened than ever.

"I used to be very nervous [all the time]. But after I started to read books to the children, it changed my way of talking and creating conversation with others. It changed me a lot."

So suddenly a talk in front of a couple hundred people, though undoubtedly a bit frightening, was just another step in her growth as an entrepreneur, teacher, community leader, poet, and advocate for girls.

"There were a lot of famous people speaking before me and in the audience. Big reporters, celebrities. I was last, and I was afraid I wouldn't know what to say. So I asked the moderator to ask me questions, rather than me giving a speech."

When the moment arrived and her name was called, Asma was ready. She walked onto the stage with a beaming smile. Asma confidently responded to questions from the moderator about Stories of the Sun, her poetry, and her other social initiatives – and the impact they were having on the children in Za'atari.

When she walked off the stage that day, it was to thunderous applause and a standing ovation. Another moment to remember in Za'atari. A symbol of the power that Asma had found within herself at the camp.

"It was the most memorable day of my life. I was so, so proud. I will never forget that day. I will never forget it."

CHAPTER 11

Global Catalyst

Refugees like Yasmina, Asma, and Malak bring immense value – economic, cultural, spiritual, and interpersonal – to their new communities, in both camps and cities alike. Since the economic element is the easiest to quantify, that is where we will begin.

In refugee camps, the economic model has traditionally been one of top-down aid. The initial assumption is that camps will be temporary shelters, so the sole focus should be on ensuring that basic resources are brought into them to sustain, heal, and protect their residents. But, as Za'atari and so many other camps exemplify, what are designed to be temporary settlements often, because of ongoing conflict back at home and resistance to full resettlement by other countries, become semipermanent. And though many do not want to admit it, there is a chance that some camps will need to live on as permanent settlements – an unideal circumstance that would symbolize a failure of resettling nations and of attempts at peacemaking in areas of conflict, but a reality nonetheless.

What is too often under-resourced and ignored, then, is what is required beyond initial emergency humanitarian response: the creation of socioeconomic opportunity. This is the pivot from just ensuring refugees are alive and safe, to also helping them rebuild their lives.

But refugee entrepreneurs, not ones to wait on the world around them to create opportunities on their behalf, are stimulating those opportunities on their own. Za'atari is a striking example. The camp's economy was built by enterprising residents working collectively to improve resource availability and families' quality of life. And, as Yasmina demonstrates, people from nearby Jordanian cities engage with camp-created ventures as customers, suppliers, and partners – so the economic gains are felt across the region.

Za'atari is not alone. Camps around the globe – from Kutupalong in Bangladesh, to Skaramagas in Greece, to Dadaab in Kenya – have emerged or begun to emerge as hubs of entrepreneurship, to the surprise of those who imagine refugees in camps as passively reliant on aid. As one Syrian refugee in Skaramagas summarized, "They've bombed our homes, jeopardized the lives of our loved ones, and forced us to endure journeys not even movies can replicate, but the one thing that is still ours and can never be taken from us is the work we produce with our God-given hands."[1]

In the Bidi Bidi refugee camp in Uganda, refugees from South Sudan have made the most of the government's increasingly relaxed rules on business creation. Bolstered by significant infrastructure improvements including the establishment of permanent schools and hospital structures, entrepreneurs – supported by the government – have created countless jobs for fellow residents and contributed to the developing economy.[2] In Dadaab, refugee entrepreneurs have built an economy generating about $25 million a year in revenue.[3] The camp has provided surrounding communities with quality goods and services, while introducing additional trading opportunities.[4] The world's largest camp, Kutupalong, has seen an emerging movement around entrepreneurship as well. As one reporter described the camp:

> [Camp residents] run roadside stalls and bustling markets. There are pop-up cinemas and venues to watch televised football matches. There are shops that sell tailor-made dresses, [play] the latest Top-40 hit, or [display] bite-sized news broadcasts for a population hungry for information. And there are entertainers-for-hire who sing joyous songs at weddings – and ballads that evoke bittersweet memories of Myanmar.[5]

Camps, then, are being transformed by refugees into communities with market ecosystems and growing economies. As aid organizations begin to take note of refugees' remarkable abilities to design new communities filled with ventures of all kinds, they have implemented programs to offer support to entrepreneurs. Increasingly, innovators like Asma, Masika in Sherkole, and Karrus in Budubaram can access the help of incubator, training, and business development programs led by NGOs like Save the Children and the Norwegian Refugee Council. These initiatives aim to further catalyze refugees' innovations, usually providing a mix of startup capital, mentoring, structure, and a community as they go about their entrepreneurial journeys. And as we saw in these cases, even minimal capital and resources – educational books for Asma, $72 for Masika, and $50 for Karrus – are enough to spur refugee entrepreneurs toward beautifully transformative ventures.

✳ — ✳ — ✳

Meanwhile, refugees have ignited significant positive change in refugee-welcoming nations and cities around the world – from Burmese, Bosnian, Somali, and dozens of other groups of refugees revitalizing the once-declining city of Utica in the US, to long-persecuted Hazara Afghan refugees creating ventures that are reinvigorating the city of Port Adelaide in Australia.

Many cities and towns have been revived in large part by refugees. American cities in the Rust Belt offer examples. With factories closing due to deindustrialization and the Great Recession, many towns were in free fall, dealing with lost jobs, declining populations, and blighted neighborhoods. Some turned to refugees as a lifeline. And many of those towns have been, at least in part, reinvigorated. In Cleveland, Ohio, refugees from different parts of the world – especially Bhutan, Myanmar, Somalia, and Ukraine – have notably advanced the economy through a combination of entrepreneurship and employment. In all, a recent study showed that refugees have "boosted the Cleveland economy by $48 million."[6] Refugee entrepreneurs have been pivotal changemakers: "[r]efugee-owned businesses directly contributed $7.6 million in economic activity to the city in just a year."[7]

Chip's adoptive town of Utica, New York – nicknamed "the town that loves refugees" – provides another lesson in what welcoming refugees can do to help revive a city and its economy. Factory shutdowns led to the exodus of one-third of Utica's population, spelling disaster for a city once projected to be among the largest in America.[8] Houses were abandoned, and small businesses shuttered.[9]

With their relentless hustle, refugees began infusing much-needed energy into Utica at a time when it looked like the ink had dried on the story of a once-burgeoning city. Thanks to large waves of resettled refugees from about thirty nations, Utica began experiencing a resurgence from its low point. Little by little, with the aid of business-boosting services like Chip's app development company, a construction company led by a Bosnian refugee that rebuilt abandoned houses, and ventures launched by many other refugee entrepreneurs, the tide started turning in Utica. The barren houses on the east side began to fill with life, the sleepy downtown was given a jolt, and declining churches began to see their congregations restored. Today, Utica is in a much more vibrant state than before. Refugees – who make up a quarter of the city's population – have brought jobs, joy, energy, and life to the Rust Belt town. Though it still suffers from its fair share of challenges, Utica's local economy has been stabilized in large part by the refugee population.

As Utica demonstrates, refugee populations infuse life, reenergize forgotten neighborhoods, and stimulate spending. Even the population support alone was critical in Utica, as locally born families were departing the town: "Without its new Bosnian community, for example, Utica would have faced a [6] percent population drop. With them, the city saw a [3] percent gain."[10] The population and economic benefits have become so clear to city halls across America that a frequent economic development strategy for declining towns is to campaign the national government to be a key receiving point for refugees. Indeed, "[e]ighteen cities in the Rust Belt alone have established programs to attract, integrate, and empower refugees."[11] And it works. One study analyzed the "11 cities that have resettled the most refugees per capita from 2005 and 2017" and found that "refugee resettlement either stemmed population loss or reversed it completely" in almost all of them.[12] Success stories abound of refugees enlivening neighborhoods across the US, in cities like Columbus, Ohio;[13] St. Louis, Missouri;[14] Oklahoma City, Oklahoma;[15] and Clarkston, Georgia.[16]

Meanwhile, on the other side of the globe in South Australia, 2,000 Hazara Afghan refugees have helped transform the city of Port Adelaide.[17] The Hazara ethnic group has dealt with among the most persistent histories of persecution, and now faces the prospect of even more attacks given the Taliban's record of targeting Hazaras.[18] About 50,000 Hazara refugees have been resettled in Australia,[19] and their entrepreneurial energy in Port Adelaide, as one example, has helped turn around a declining city. The lead author of a report by two universities in the region explained that Hazara refugees "have revitalised Port Adelaide in countless ways," noting the city's newfound economic strength thanks to myriad refugee-owned small businesses in areas ranging from real estate, to construction, to food, and beyond.[20] The author also highlighted the discrepancy between how refugees are portrayed and the powerful impact they have made on the region:

> Negative media reports have portrayed refugees and asylum seekers as a burden, cost or threat to Australian communities, but all the research points to the opposite . . . . Port Adelaide was in decline 15 years ago but the Hazara migrants have helped to transform the area into a thriving, multicultural, dynamic hub.[21]

Moreover, refugees are accomplishing all this in spite of identified barriers to integration in Port Adelaide, including job discrimination and social isolation. On the positive side, however, several efforts of the Port Adelaide community have been credited in helping refugees assimilate – from housing support, to translation services, to sports and community education centers.[22]

The same economic benefits experienced by Utica and Port Adelaide can be seen in host cities where refugees are not as often permanently resettled, but are temporarily allowed to live in local communities. As one example, Turkey, Jordan, Iraq, Lebanon, and Egypt have allowed significant numbers of Syrian refugees to live in their cities, at least temporarily. In Egypt, Syrian refugees have infused $800 million of contributions into the national economy.[23] There, Syrian entrepreneurs "have turned the neighborhoods of 6th of October City . . . into bustling corridors of

Syrian restaurants and grocery stores to the point that the area is now called 'Little Damascus.'"[24] Meanwhile, in 2017 alone, Turkey saw the founding of more than 8,000 new Syrian companies;[25] since 2013, 10 percent of new businesses established in Turkey were by Syrians, and on average each of these businesses employs several people.[26]

Make no mistake, there is an economic cost to welcoming refugees. But that investment easily reaps dividends in the form of business growth, increased hiring, higher spending, a broader tax base, and beyond. Ultimately, the investment is a clear winner for welcoming nations, and even more so when refugees are appropriately integrated and supported. Consider the conclusion of the US Department of Health and Human Services's 2017 draft report on the subject, which was ultimately left unpublished by the Trump administration: "Overall, this report estimated that the net fiscal impact of refugees [in the US] was positive over the 10-year period [between 2005 and 2014], at $63 billion."[27] Similarly in Europe, one report projected that the cohorts of refugees fleeing to the European Union in 2015 and 2016 alone could "deliver a positive overall GDP contribution of about €60 billion to €70 billion annually if the refugees are integrated into the labor market and society."[28]

Put directly, the economic contributions of refugees vastly outweigh the costs of welcoming them, and even more so when they are welcomed with strong support structures in place.

Speaking only of economics, of course, does not fully capture the quiet moments of love, comfort, and together- ness created by refugees' very presence as neighbors, col- leagues, and friends in communities around the world. Entrepreneurship itself, and refugee entrepreneurship in particular, is about so much more than dollars and cents.

Refugee-led businesses are often the lifeblood of their communities. They infuse a diversity and intercultural understanding that shapes new relationships, and produces new enrichment opportunities. As the commissioner of Utica's Department of Urban and Economic Development told CNBC: "The refugee population has helped the city's economy tremendously, not only adding to the quality of life but also the diversity of our neighborhoods and schools, as well as to the diversity of our retail business offerings."[29] In Utica, more than forty languages are represented in the public schools; children enjoy the benefit of an exceptional multicultural experience just by going to algebra class.[30]

Refugees also give back as mentors and supporters of the business communities in their adoptive homes, often with a heightened sense of loyalty to the places that wel- comed them. Faith, a political refugee from Zimbabwe who opposed the Robert Mugabe regime, dealt with several periods of homelessness in Nottingham, England as she applied for asylum and was rejected several times. After eight years, she was finally granted refugee status by the government and, within days, was actively seeking funding for her business idea. Today, thanks in part to support from foundations and incubators, she both runs a clothing com- pany featuring African-print dresses from across the continent and assists others in starting their own businesses.[31] As she described her mission to the Entrepreneurial Refugee Network, "I want to empower other refugees and asylum-seekers from the African community by giving them textiles and leadership skills at my company."[32]

Meanwhile, Razan of Yorkshire Dama Cheese is popular among the other cheese company leaders in the region, as she has helped expand and diversify the cheese market: "I am in very good relations with the other cheesemakers in the UK. They don't look at me as a competitor. They look at me as someone who is completing the cheese family in the UK."[33] Chip, too, could have taken her talents anywhere in the US and changed her home base, but she remained committed to the central New York town that raised her, helping modernize small businesses in the area.

Additionally, refugee social entrepreneurs directly transform the lives of residents through their work, with social good as their primary mission. Asma's storytelling initiative is a prime example of a purely social venture. Other hybrid models have dual bottom lines of profit and social impact. Seeba, for example, was launched by three Syrian social entrepreneurs – Maha, Omran, and Yasser – who were resettled in Toronto, Canada. A social enterprise painting company, Seeba aims to provide high-quality painting services to homes and businesses. Its other goal is to level the playing field in terms of opportunity and equal pay for women, minorities, and refugees by actively seeking to recruit these often-marginalized groups. As is commonly the case, these three entrepreneurs were supported by incubators in their new home country, which offered a free website, digital marketing services, and other useful tools.[34]

Importantly, though this book is specifically about refugees who are entrepreneurs, the contributions of refugee communities more generally shine brightly. There is tremendous value created by refugees who live, work, volunteer, play, and commune in places around the world.

Refugees revive the spiritual hearts of towns. Many churches in America, for example, have been rejuvenated by refugees. Churches like the 162-year-old Zion Lutheran in Iowa, where a congregation that was once mostly homogeneous transformed to become 50 percent minority in composition when its leadership welcomed refugees from dozens of communities.[35] As its pastor has proudly noted, the congregation now worships in four languages and prays in at least twelve languages.[36] Or like Tabernacle Church in Utica, which was on its last leg until it was rejuvenated by an influx of refugees. It now welcomes more than 1,000 congregation members from the persecuted Karen ethnic groups in Myanmar, and in 2018 named its newly refurbished steeple in honor of them.[37] Nearby in downtown Utica, a historic abandoned church in a prominent location was repurposed into a mosque by the many Bosnian refugees who settled in the town. The mosque's opening was celebrated at a community meeting filled with heartfelt support and appreciation, sometimes most passionately voiced by those who had once attended the church years prior.[38]

Refugees are also compassionate community members in times of emergency, heartbreak, and loss.

During the COVID-19 pandemic, refugees have selflessly taken leads as frontline workers, makers of protective and medical equipment, and beyond. Fezzeh, a refugee doctor from Afghanistan, has served as the head of her Iranian province's COVID-19 public outreach program. Recognizing an increase in domestic violence during the pandemic, she has also led group calls focused on health and personal support with Afghan women and girls.[39] In Kutupalong, a team of 1,400 Rohingya refugees served as trained door-to-door community health workers, sharing critical health guidance and referring potential COVID-19 patients to the camp's clinics.[40] One Burundian soap maker in the Kakuma camp named Innocent responded to the pandemic by dropping his prices so that everyone in the camp could be protected.[41]

Before, during, and after Hurricane Harvey devastated Houston in 2017, the city's significant refugee population was active in helping its adoptive community stay safe and recover over time. Amidst the devastation, many heartwarming stories emerged. Volunteers from the Afghan Cultural Center, for example, "helped firefighters whose truck was stuck in the street use their hose so they could put out a house fire[,] . . . distributed supplies, helped people get their belongings to higher areas and moved families to safe places."[42]

Dayana, a twenty-eight-year-old Syrian woman who was set to celebrate her one-year anniversary in America, would check on her neighbors between trips to grocery stores in preparation for the storm. As she told a reporter by phone:

> I am so sad, because I love Houston and I love all the people here[.] [T]he people here are so nice, I just hope

everything is [okay]. Don't forget to pray for us – and maybe when this is done, you can come visit me and we can make Arabic food.[43]

An Afghan refugee named Nisar echoed the sentiment: "These people welcome us ... and ... accept us here in the United States, and we feel proud that we helped [those in need during Hurricane Harvey]. As ... human[s], we help them."[44]

Nisar's quote is a reminder that even more fundamental than their economic, social, and other contributions, refugees are – above all – just that: humans. They are mothers, fathers, sons, daughters, and friends. Discussions about refugee entrepreneurship naturally lend themselves toward the impact refugees make, but that impact is not the primary reason refugees should matter to us; refugees should matter to us simply because of *who they are* ... fundamentally equal people who deserve to be treated with full respect, dignity, and love, just the same as everyone else.

Now, with a sense for what refugees *are* in their new communities, there remains an important question: what are they *not*? Despite dangerous rhetoric that seems to have increasingly taken hold in recent years, they are not causing spikes in crime. The New American Economy closely studied this issue, reviewing Federal Bureau of Investigation (FBI) crime statistics in the US among the ten cities that resettled the most refugees as a proportion of their populations between 2006 and 2015. The results were straightforward: safety improved. The report notes:

> In nine of the 10 cities, both violent and property crime rates fell [after the resettlement of refugees], in some

cases, dramatically. The one city that saw crime increase was battling a well-documented opioid epidemic during this same period.[45]

Ultimately, then, while the "victim" narrative about refugees is incomplete in that only a part of refugees' stories is about their losses and hardships, the "villain" narrative about refugees is simply inaccurate.

————*

"Refugee" is a word that carries with it all kinds of connotations and images – often political and divisive ones. That may be truer today than ever before.

Amidst the largest global refugee crisis in history, most of us know refugees only from the media headlines ... children in boats on the Mediterranean, women in Central American caravans, families waiting in lines at European borders. As we have seen, some view refugees as merely victims: objects of pity. Others view them as villains: unwelcome disruptors threatening to tear at their adoptive nations' moral fabric. Either way, we don't often get the opportunity to see them as whole human beings – the way one might see Yasmina when sewing a wedding dress, or Asma when holding her child, or Malak when discussing her art.

In part because of this binary view of refugees, countries – to their own detriment – are too often reluctant to welcome them and invest in helping them plant their feet on solid ground. As many refugee entrepreneurs' stories demonstrate, there are commendable efforts in a number of camps and cities to uplift and integrate refugees. All 193 UN member nations have agreed to work toward this end, and some nations are improving in allowing refugees to legally work.[46] But the global effort has been sorely insufficient in providing meaningful opportunities to refugee families. And the failure to provide these opportunities starts early, as refugee children today remain "five times more likely to be out of school than non-refugee children."[47]

Moreover, there is a sizable sentiment on the side of denying refugees entry into nations and cities altogether. When asked about refugees from Syria in an opinion poll in 2015, 64 percent of Americans were against the idea of accepting any Syrian refugees at all or were in favor of only accepting Christians, a group desperately in need of relief but still just a minority of those displaced from the country.[48] These poll respondents are, in effect, saying no to Malak, no to Asma, and no to Yasmina – three women who any one of the respondents would surely be honored to have in their communities if they knew them.

⁎——⁎——⁎

There is a lot of noise surrounding the topic of refugees. But through the rubble of the refugee crisis emerges a fuller, brighter story. A story of finding life, and home, even in the midst of agonizing loss. A story of resilient, vibrant innovation. It is an entrepreneurial story of hope – the untold story of refugee entrepreneurs.

The truth is that beyond the fray – the talking heads, the eye-catching headlines, and the viral videos – are quiet moments of humanity experienced by refugees and their communities around the world. Quiet moments of hope, of joy, and of resilience. Moments of dignity.

Two thousand years ago, an author believed to be the Apostle Paul wrote a letter extolling the early Christian church to be welcoming to strangers: "Do not neglect to show hospitality to strangers, for thereby some have entertained angels unawares."[49]

The world's refugee story is not about letting past disasters determine people's futures; it is about uplifting and investing in underdogs harboring big dreams.

The world's refugee story is not solely about economic value; it is about the quiet moments of love and unity playing out every day in our communities.

The world's refugee story is not about the exclusion of the downtrodden; it is about the welcoming of angels.

Part IV

Hope

Hold fast to dreams
For if dreams die
Life is a broken-winged bird
That cannot fly.
—Langston Hughes, "Dreams"

CHAPTER 12

Dreams Become One

It's still pitch dark, before dawn in Za'atari. Before the horses draw the carts of vegetables to the Shams-Élysées; before the trailer shutters are unlocked and opened; before the children walk to school with their textbooks in hand, playfully pushing one another down the street. The only light and the only stirring at this moment is coming from Trailer 6.4, District 8.

The last time Asma couldn't sleep like this was teacher training day.

But today is a special day for very different reasons. Asma and her family have an appointment in Amman – an interview at the Canadian embassy. They had applied for resettlement months ago and were recently notified of the meeting.

Tamara, Maya, and their younger sister Madelyn emerge from the back room of the trailer in matching seafoam green dresses, their hair done up. Carrying Mohammed with them, they are ready to go and on time, as promised, so that the family can arrive at their appointment promptly.

The four of them are the reason for all of this, Asma shares. They deserve more consistent, higher quality education. "I want Tamara to be a lawyer. Of course, my children will choose their careers. But I want a better future for them than what they have here." Increasingly, the odds of resettlement are slim. So Asma knows this is a significant opportunity. She is a bit nervous, only because she wants to put the family's best foot forward in the interview. She wants to do everything in her power to create a future for her kids way beyond anything she could have ever dreamt of.

As she steps foot through the wooden door that countless children from all around Za'atari have tumbled through, she looks back at the sign in front of her home: قصص للشمس, Stories of the Sun. Asma has poured her heart into this place. If everything lined up for a move to Canada, she would of course do it . . . but with a heavy heart. Perhaps she would leave it to Nawara to take over the storytelling initiative; she has proven herself to be a more-than-capable heir apparent.

But no reason to get ahead of herself. There is no way to tell what the future holds, just as there was no way she could have predicted her life would take her to this place. Before she walks into the quiet Za'atari morning, Asma simply says to herself with a sense of peace:

"In shah Allah."

"God willing."

⚹ —— ⚹ —— ⚹

Deepest in the hearts of most in Za'atari is the desire to go home. That there will be lasting peace in Syria and that they can return once and for all. That they can be among the familiar ... the family, friends, and olive trees once more. Second is the desire for a chance to resettle somewhere with greater opportunities for their children.

This is doubly true when it comes to the older generations – the people who spent most of their adult lives in Syria and remember the types of opportunities a stable home can provide when compared to Za'atari. They only left, after all, because they had little or no choice. As the Somali British poet Warsan Shire eloquently wrote, "no one leaves home unless / home is the mouth of a shark," "no one puts their children in a boat / unless the water is safer than the land," and "no one chooses refugee camps."[1]

Count Yasmina as one whose eyes are set on home: "Everyone wants to go back. But only when things get better." Unfortunately, the Syrian war, now beyond the decade mark, has outlasted all timeline predictions so far. The conflict that began with graffiti in Dara'a has escalated into one of the most disastrous conflicts in modern history.

But optimism is part of how Yasmina stayed alive with a neighborhood crashing down upon her. Optimism is part of how she managed to make it to Za'atari while pregnant with Ashraf, ensuring he stayed alive and was born into safety. Optimism is part of how she launched the Salon of Lights, first as a small project in her trailer and then into the most dynamic store in Saudi Market. And optimism is part of how she helped transform Za'atari by spreading joy and celebration throughout the dusty streets and corrugated metal trailers.

The optimism she harbors is not easy, but she knows it is not solely for her. It is for her children. "My hope for my kids is that they are educated. That they can improve their lives for the better."

"In shah Allah, things will get better."

❊——❊——❊

The reasons Asma and Yasmina seek to leave Za'atari – to return back home or, alternatively, to resettle to a place of peace and opportunity for their children – are obvious. Despite the incredible people of Za'atari and the progress they have catalyzed in the camp itself, there is no ignoring the daily challenges of camp life.

Progress has been made in education, but not enough. This is where Asma and Yasmina center their hopes of leaving: they long for their children to have access to better-quality education. Children and youth aged seventeen or under make up about 56 percent of the total residents of Za'atari.[2] More than thirty schools have been built in Za'atari, and humanitarian organizations like UNICEF and Save the Children – in partnership with trained Za'atari teachers like Asma – operate a number of additional informal education, training, and enrichment programs.[3] Enrollment of the school-age population has gone up to more than 70 percent – now including about 20,000 children – to mark a major improvement from the early days of the camp.[4] Still, the enrollment rate lags behind global rates, and too many children do not attend school because they are instead working to help provide for the basic needs of their families.[5] And even the children now enrolled in school face the tough road of catching up on the critical time they missed, which requires additional support.[6]

Progress has been made in health care, but not enough. Several hospitals and health care centers have been established, and hard-working clinicians engage in thousands of health consultations a week.[7] One key initiative, especially given many residents' mobility impairments and accessibility issues, is the deployment of community health volunteers to travel to families' trailers to provide care, including various types of therapies.[8] Volunteers like these, most of whom are Za'atari residents, are also critical given limited capacity at the camp's hospitals and health care centers.[9] But camp residents still struggle. Sometimes, they relay these struggles to aid workers, hoping that things might change for the better. One pizza restaurant owner, for example, shared the story of his daughter who died due to a lack of adequate cancer treatment; though she was no longer with him, he wanted to ensure that this tragedy did not befall any other fathers in Za'atari. Moreover, mental health services continue to be inadequate – especially for a community whose circumstances lend themselves to such high levels of anxiety.[10]

Progress has been made in terms of inclusivity for those with disabilities, but not enough. One powerful example is the addition of Za'atari's inclusive playground. Led by UNICEF and Mercy Corps in Jordan, and supported by the governments of South Korea, England, and Australia, the playground has tailored equipment that allows children with mobility impairments to participate in group physical activity.[11] It is "the first fully inclusive playground for children with disabilities" ever implemented in a refugee camp.[12] The effort's goal is to provide the hundreds of children with disabilities who attend UNICEF-supported schools with a place for belonging, physical activity, and fun.[13] Creating more enrichment spaces like this for children with disabilities is critical to sustaining their mental and physical health, and generating a spirit of hope, community, and equality in Za'atari.

Finally, progress has been made in human rights and protection of residents, but not enough. Campaigns like the one Malak helped lead have raised awareness about child marriage and the numbers appear to have declined significantly,[14] but it remains an issue that needs to be fully addressed.

Solutions to these issues and progress toward peace itself – as Malak, Yasmina, and Asma illustrate – are far more powerful and sustainable when led by refugees themselves, in particular refugee women. 2011 Nobel Peace Prize Laureate Leymah Gbowee lived in a refugee camp in Ghana before returning to her home of Liberia and leading a nonviolent peace movement that united Christian and Muslim women. With insight born of experience in helping guide Liberia toward remarkable peace after more than a decade of war, she explained:

> Refugee women are not passive victims; they are strong and courageous leaders, often the first ones to respond to

the needs of their community . . . . The best thing we can do for refugee communities is to provide them – especially women and girls – with opportunities to create the change they need . . . . When we let ourselves be led by refugee women and girls, we will create real change in the lives of refugees.[15]

✳——❊——❧

Then there are the younger generations, who have spent all or a large portion of their formative years in Za'atari. Who see it as, in many ways, their hometown. This is Malak's generation.

Yes, Malak still seeks first and foremost to go home. "I love Syria. I hope I will return one day to my country, with its peace and freedoms. We lost peace in our small country."

But Malak hopes that, even if she is to remain in Za'atari for long, it will be better resourced so that all children and youths will have the opportunity to realize their God-given gifts. She accepts her life in Za'atari for now and sees her new purpose as living out her gifts boldly in the camp, acting as a role model for the children around her.

"In shah Allah, I will finish my bachelor's degree and get my master's degree. My biggest dream for my art . . . is I would love to have my own separate studio with a garden area to help me draw and paint. And a gallery to show my art to others."

One painting, in particular, symbolizes that hope. It is of a woman with her eyes cast upward. In Malak's signature style, the painting mixes vibrant colors representing

optimism for the future and darker shades to acknowledge the difficulty of the current reality.

"The painting has dark colors around [the left side of] her face to signify sadness, but it moves toward brighter colors to signify her moving from darkness to light."

Malak learned from Asma and others who are older than her, who in turn learned from Yasmina and the generation above. All three are women who faced the gravest of obstacles, but rose to meet them with leadership, grace, and courage. To them, the word "refugee" is at once a source of immense pain and a badge of great honor. And it's just one component of who they are. They are three dynamic entrepreneurs striving to uplift their devastated communities. Three compassionate mentors seeking to empower the next generation the way they had to fight to empower themselves. Three powerful leaders who will not let Za'atari be a place merely of sorrow or of pain or of darkness. Three of the brightest lights, illuminating the world around them.

Angels of Za'atari, to be sure. As usual, Asma has a way with her words:

We were afraid we might bury our dreams under the ground,
But we didn't lose hope, and we promised we will never lose it.
After we settled in Za'atari, we encouraged each other,
So our dreams remain as a light to clear our way to our future.

Because we are strong in unity together,
Our thoughts and our dreams become one.[16]

EPILOGUE

Asma, Malak, and Yasmina are three examples of a reality that is hopefully apparent from this book: refugees are some of the most resilient, brave, and inspiring human beings on this planet. Emerging from our global crisis are some of the world's most remarkable stories: refugees turning unimaginable pain into beautiful reinvention. These refugee entrepreneurs and their families remind us that people are multidimensional, and often so much more than how they are portrayed. Moreover, they offer a source of hope for social progress and a grassroots model for global economic development – offering the potential to transform crises into major opportunities.

So how do we best tangibly support refugees – in camps and in cities – to get back on their feet and use their talents, kindness, and generosity to uplift communities around them? I don't purport to know anything near the full answer, but the type of narrative change contemplated in this book is one fundamental step to catalyzing more concrete action.

From the media coverage about refugees in camps, you might see the residents as hopeless masses merely biding their time without hope. From articles and some politicians' speeches about refugees who have fled temporarily to host countries or have been formally resettled in new countries, you might think that the refugee crisis is nothing but a massive drain on national economies. In recent years and continuing today, we have seen debates within nations all over the world about whether it should be their duty to "shoulder the economic burden" of relocating refugees – not to mention the supposed risk of introducing crime and cultural decay.

Refugees faced immensely difficult conditions in being forced out of their homes through no fault of their own. Those in camps are thankful to have been granted a place to stay, but underfunded facilities make life unfathomably hard for families often still shaking from the trauma of departure. So, yes, there is great importance in telling the harrowing stories of the challenges faced by refugees, as this book aims to do in Part I, to awaken the world to the injustices they face. And yes, for those countries temporarily hosting or resettling refugees, there is a real economic cost. But one-dimensional narratives like these overlook the fact that refugees seeking a new life are a valuable source of innovation and economic growth, and – most importantly – are equal human beings who deserve full respect, independent of their contributions. In refugee camps, they are building communities and businesses from scratch, turning what many would expect to be a singularly dark place into one with some joy and light. In towns and cities, they are helping fellow refugees while also supporting native-born communities, introducing them to new cultures, supporting them during times of community crisis, and employing many of them with their creative ventures – while not introducing the dangers and risks some irresponsibly warn about.

164

Most fundamentally, this narrative shift is critical to recognize and respect the equal dignity of refugee families around the world. Such a step is powerful and required in and of itself. Rather than being viewed as only victims or as villains, refugees should be viewed as whole human beings. Equal human beings with inherent worth, who are no worse or better than anyone else.

Even beyond that inherent value, the narrative shift is pivotal to mobilizing resources and support in a way that tangibly enables refugees to use their abilities to change their own lives and their communities' lives. If refugees are mistakenly viewed as helpless, lazy, or crime-prone, decision-makers and leaders are less likely to channel capital and assistance to them – aside from perhaps basic humanitarian aid. If they are viewed more accurately as innovators, greater investment and support will be deployed to making their ideas work. Refugees should be seen as the assets they are, not as liabilities.

The next piece of the puzzle, then, is the set of initiatives that invest in and support refugees' business and social enterprise ideas – all of which must complement existing aid that helps refugees meet their essential needs. Though stories about refugee entrepreneurs are left mostly untold in the general media, they are beginning to catch the attention of organizations that seek to both create opportunities for those who are disadvantaged and to generate economic growth. Their initiatives perform two functions, with many doing a bit of both: mobilizing capital to invest in and support refugee-led ideas, and providing on-the-ground support for those ideas. We are beginning to see a recent, budding trend of organizations marshaling financial and programmatic resources to support a group that is usually excluded from both.

As for mobilizing much-needed capital to equip refugees in camps and cities with the resources to create new ideas, there is a small-but-growing "refugee investment" movement. For the organizations involved, the rationale is simple: if refugee entrepreneurs are doing all of this amazing work against the steepest of odds, despite the most difficult life circumstances, with almost no support . . . imagine what they could do with even a fraction of the support provided to emerging entrepreneurs in better resourced communities. These organizations recognize the immense, life-saving value of humanitarian aid to ensure that refugees have what they need to survive, but also recognize the need to go above and beyond to create sustainable solutions. With the knowledge that the true image of refugees is not as the victims devoid of agency that they are often portrayed as, these groups rightfully view their infusions of capital as money going to responsible and entrepreneurial individuals . . . individuals who will turn that capital into jobs, economic activity, and more capital – not to mention joy, community, and mutual understanding across cultures.

One leader in this nascent movement has been Kiva, a crowd-lending platform that serves financially excluded entrepreneurs around the world. Its CEO described the need to mobilize capital to support refugees in launching and sustaining their own ventures:

> Refugees and displaced populations often live in their
> new host communities for several years, but struggle to

find work, start businesses or re-establish a source of income for their families. The situation calls for a paradigm shift towards new, sustainable solutions that can both help the displaced and support the communities that host them.

Partnering with the UNHCR and local financial institutions across the globe, Kiva launched the World Refugee Fund in 2017 to deliver loans to refugee entrepreneurs. In evaluating its distribution of more than $14 million to nearly 18,000 refugees, Kiva's conclusions are what you might expect based on the distinctive qualities of refugee entrepreneurs described in Chapter 8: they are incredibly reliable, with a repayment rate of 95.5 percent.[1] I have personally seen the same power of investing in refugee entrepreneurs through the partnership between my organization – DreamxAmerica – and Kiva US, which has so far connected immigrant, refugee, and first-generation entrepreneurs in the US to more than $200,000 in crowd-lent, zero-interest loans during the COVID-19 pandemic. Beyond our entrepreneurs' 100 percent repayment rate so far and their businesses' local economic impact, we have seen that they – despite hailing from more than twenty different nations and living in cities across America – are unified by something special: a deeply felt desire to serve their communities. Virtually all entrepreneurs we work with talk about using their skills, first and foremost, to *help others* – a beautiful, powerful, and selfless thing, especially given how difficult it has been for small business owners during the pandemic.

Attempting to develop an underlying infrastructure to enable these investments to be more than isolated springs of lending support – but instead embedded within investment practice more broadly – is the Refugee Investment Network. The organization is working to mobilize investment capital to refugee-led ventures by designing tailored evaluation tools for investors seeking to fund refugee-led businesses and cultivating a coalition of interested investors.[2] This work helps to create a framework for greater investment in refugees, though in the end investment institutions must step up to the plate by making a real effort to source and fund refugee-led businesses.

Meanwhile, to complement the work done to raise capital for refugee entrepreneurs, the ground-level support is perhaps just as critical. There are many programmatic partners doing excellent work to support refugee entrepreneurs in camps and cities. In host cities, one example organization called Al Majmoua has worked to build both economic growth and mutual understanding in Lebanon. It provides loans to groups of women composed of both Syrian refugees and Lebanese residents, creating opportunities for these two communities – which could otherwise feel as though they were in tension – to advance their local areas together.[3] Recall that Razan, the founder and CEO of Yorkshire Dama Cheese, had no way of starting her venture until a UK government program provided her mentorship along with a £2,500 loan. And remember, too, the two Canadian incubators that supported the launch of Seeba, the painting services social enterprise that focuses on employing marginalized communities.

This type of field-level support can have pivotal results. In the Ecuadorian province of Esmeraldas, which hosts thousands of refugees and asylum seekers mostly from Colombia, a UNCHR partnership with the Pontifical

Catholic University of Ecuador has supported refugee entrepreneurs since 2011. The two organizations launched an
incubator that provides training on accounting, market
assessment, and other business administration fundamen-
tals. The partnership has observed that, compared to the
general 95 percent two-year failure rate of businesses in
Esmeraldas, businesses supported by the incubator have a
failure rate of just 15 percent.[4] Migration Hub, itself founded
by an immigrant, offers development space, training, and
education to immigrant and refugee entrepreneurs in countries across the Middle East and Europe.[5] And Five One Labs
supports refugees who come from conflict areas of the
Middle East with an agile-focused approach: training on
the lean startup methodology, offering pitch competitions,
and coordinating hackathons to raise as many compelling
ideas to the surface as quickly as possible.[6]

In camps, several humanitarian NGOs are making
the pivot to go beyond emergency aid, adding in self-
sustaining initiatives that include entrepreneurial support.
This has increasingly become the case as aid organizations
and the world have realized that, sadly, many camps are
facing the reality of longer existences than they were
intended for. In Za'atari, we saw the Design Squad Club's
STEM program and We Love Reading's support for social
entrepreneurs and teachers with a desire to improve the lives
of children. Recall that in Sherkole, Masika's initial $72 of
funding from the Norwegian Refugee Council spurred the
launch of her restaurant and baking startup. We also saw
how Karrus's education initiatives in the Budubaram camp
were catalyzed by the support of a local church and a $50

loan. There are many more examples around the world of incubator and small-business development programs in refugee camps, most of them supported by international NGOs with a presence in those camps.

These many efforts have established a helpful blueprint for the future, beginning to pave the two critical paths: mobilization of capital and on-the-ground venture support. Unfortunately, the reality is that these developments are all too rare, and many of them have begun to emerge only in recent years. Governments and businesses with courage could mobilize dramatically more financial resources to help refugees get settled and launch successful businesses, in turn seeing a major economic and societal return on investment for everyone. And taking the lead from grassroots initiatives that are already working with usually very limited funding, we need to partner across sectors to emphasize identification and development of ventures as well as training of refugee entrepreneurs – establishing incubators, teaching basic business skills, and offering mentorship from veteran entrepreneurs in every camp and city where refugees live.

Ultimately, then, there is much work left to be done to design a future that creates inclusive economic growth focused on welcoming refugees and supporting their ideas. And there is no more important time than now to act.

❋ — ❋ — ❋

How can we as individuals help in this path to socioeconomic opportunity for refugees? First, and most simply, support begins at home. If there are refugees in your home-town or community, be a proactive welcoming and support-ive presence. Offer to support them in any way you can, and help connect them to resources in your community – from refugee resettlement groups to language courses to incubator programs to trustworthy sources of lending. Remember, when someone is a stranger in an entirely new place, even a warm "welcome" and a person to go to with questions can legitimately help change the course of a family's life.

Second, funds. If you, your company, your faith institution, or your community group are willing and able to give to support refugees, it would contribute to filling the major gap that exists today. By purchasing this book, you participated in that effort in a small way, as a significant portion of proceeds is being contributed to support refugee entrepreneurs in Za'atari and around the world. You might also consider donating to aid organizations that operate or serve in refugee camps – like the UNHCR, UNICEF, the Norwegian Refugee Council, Save the Children, Mercy Corps, and Catholic Relief Services – and to other organiza-tions that work to ensure basic resources are met and entre-preneurial initiatives are fostered, including many of the examples described in this book. Closer to home, you might contribute to your regional refugee resettlement agency or immigrant welcoming center. These organizations and their usually under-resourced staffs are at the frontlines of refugee resettlement, helping refugees find places to stay and sources of lending. Recall Balighah, who found that the encourage-ment and training from a refugee resettlement center in Utica changed her life. Relatedly on the local funding front, purchasing from refugee-led businesses in your community is another way to show support.

Beyond this book's focus on entrepreneurship but important to note is the need to more appropriately support refugees who seek to enter the workforce as employees. Each of us can push for changes in our organizations to ensure they are proactively improving their recruitment, interviewing, and hiring processes – that they are not discriminating against refugees and instead are actively seeking their employment. Refugee staffing agencies like Amplio Recruiting in the US demonstrate that those companies that hire large numbers of refugees see improvements in retention and productivity – two crucial performance indicators for businesses.[7] And once again, even beyond the economic value that refugees create, it is crucial to remember that all people and families deserve a real opportunity and the chance to experience the dignity of work.

Finally, there is a need to advocate for more systemic change. One area in particular stands out in light of this book's significant focus on a refugee camp: refugee resettlement. As discussed in Part I, refugee resettlement dropped dramatically in recent years. Moreover, the programs to support refugees when they arrive in the US were wiped out at record pace – so much so that NPR called 2018 "The Year the U.S. Refugee Resettlement Program Unraveled."[8] Advocating for local, state, and national governments to establish inclusive policies that welcome refugees will be critical to ensuring the tides turn, so that people like Asma, Malak, Yasmina, and their families can have the chance to settle somewhere more permanently and with greater opportunities.

In the midst of this historic moment, we as a global community have the opportunity to become a part of the stories of refugee entrepreneurs igniting sparks in some of the darkest circumstances. We have the chance to help catalyze a movement that recognizes the gifts refugees provide to their communities, economic and beyond, and enables them to uplift those communities through their creativity, energy, and perseverance. And we should seize that chance. Because at stake is not just the dignity and opportunity of the millions of refugees in camps and cities around the world – it is the collective dignity and opportunity of our generation.

ACKNOWLEDGMENTS

My deepest gratitude and appreciation first go to the three featured entrepreneurs in Za'atari, who are the stars of this book: Asma, Malak, and Yasmina. Each welcomed me kindly into her home and was gracious in spending time telling me her story. This book does not do their stories justice; they are three of the most warm, inspiring, and powerful individuals I have ever met. There are also many other wonderful entrepreneurs I interviewed in Za'atari to whom I owe an enormous thanks, especially Eman and Malwa.

Those relationships would not have been made possible without the wonderful team at Save the Children Jordan. The staff helped ensure my permit and entry into Za'atari was sponsored, and facilitated my introductions to Asma, Malak, Yasmina, Eman, Malwa, and others. They asked for nothing in return. The team was led by the amazing Layal Twal and Sherbel Dissi, who were kind enough to help coordinate my visit and welcome me when I arrived in Amman. While in Za'atari, several additional Save the Children staff members were supportive. Although I have comfort with Arabic, primarily in the Egyptian dialect because my parents were born and raised in Egypt, translator support was critical to get to a deeper level of discussion. Sherbel was the primary translator, with Layal and Hossam stepping in for a couple of interviews. The interviews were audio recorded, and my wonderful mother, Afaf Y. Hanna, helped with more detailed translation from back home in the US. Rufut, a security guard on staff with Save the Children, helped contact entrepreneurs, coordinate meetings, and lead us to the right locations. There were several other caring staff members who supported this work, including Rafeef, Barrea, and Faris.

I also want to thank the many community leaders who welcomed me during my visit to Utica, New York, which is featured in this book as an example of an adoptive community greatly impacted by refugees. These individuals are described more comprehensively in the Notes, but a special appreciation is owed to John Bartle, Kath Stam, and Chris Sunderlin for their warmth and kindness.

Secondary sources were critical to this book – in particular regarding the reporting of facts on the ground in Syria and the stories of several of the entrepreneurs outside Za'atari. Regarding the Syrian war and in particular its effect on Dara'a, contemporary reporting of the late Anthony Shadid for *The New York Times* was invaluable. Regarding refugee entrepreneurs around the world, a number of sources were helpful, especially the work of the UNHCR in documenting entrepreneurs' stories.

I could not have asked for a better publisher to partner with than Cambridge University Press. It has been an honor to collaborate with the oldest publishing house in the world. The team I worked with – especially Lisa Carter, Chloe Bradley, Toby Ginsberg, Muhammad Ridwaan, Margaret Christie, and Chris Burrows – was exceptionally kind, thorough, engaging, and committed. A special shout-out goes to Valerie Appleby, my editor, who was a true joy to partner with at every step of the way. Her passion, empathy, and attention to detail were a main reason why I selected Cambridge, and I am glad that I did. Along the lines of the publishing process, I also owe gratitude to a veteran in the industry, Deneen Howell, who advised me at every step of the way and provided early and formative perspectives on my book proposal.

This book benefited from many others who read drafts of its various components. In an Independent Writing course with Martha Minow while I was at Harvard Law School, I refined my initial proposal and created drafts of other writing about asylum law in the US that was helpful to leverage. In my Disability Rights Law course with Michael Ashley Stein, I wrote on the experiences of people with disabilities in Za'atari, which was again useful to weave into this book. Very helpful feedback on the book or components of it came from many colleagues, friends, and family members. These included Layal Twal, Lamis Aljasem, Anny Dow, Seth Norris, Sherif Ayoub, Raquel Helen Silva, Vincent Li, Danny Mammo, Hodan Mohamoud, Riley Hawkins, Tre Holloway, Rohit G. Agarwal, Nick Bashour, Amanda Greco, Sarah Rutherford, David Delaney Mayer, Memme Onwudiwe, Izzy Macquarrie, Amorette Hanna, Amy Hanna, Afaf Y. Hanna, and Nosshey F. Hanna.

The book's development in its early stages was aided as well by the *Financial Times* and McKinsey Bracken Bower Prize. A rare competition that is aimed at supporting young authors under the age of thirty-five, the Bracken Bower Prize was a major boost to me when I received the honor in

November 2018 in London – both financially through its monetary prize to support my research and in terms of encouragement. I would recommend anyone under the age of thirty-five – no matter your previous experience in writing – to apply for the award if they have an idea that relates, even broadly, to business or economic growth.

Ultimately, the greatest appreciation I have for this book and for everything else in my life comes down to my faith and my family. I thank God for the opportunity to write this and to attempt to share a vision of equal dignity and inclusion. I believe the welcoming, support, love, and equal treatment of refugee families is as in tune with the heart of the Christian faith and the life of Jesus as any topic, and this belief is much of what inspired me to write this book and to pursue my other work related to immigrant and refugee communities. I owe everything to my parents, Dr. Nosshey F. and Afaf Y. Hanna, for sacrificing so much to put me in positions to succeed, and inspiring me with their story of immigrating to the US from Egypt. I, as always, send my deepest appreciation to them and my two sisters, Amy and Amorette, for their unconditional love.

NOTES

Quotes: All quotes in *25 Million Sparks* from Asma, Malak, and Yasmina – with the exception of those from the radio interview with Malak, as cited – are from author-conducted interviews. Accordingly, note reference markers are not placed when telling these three entrepreneurs' stories in order to avoid repetition and improve readability. All other quotes, both those from author-conducted interviews and from secondary sources, are designated with note reference markers and cited below.

Placement of Note Reference Markers: In cases where multiple sentences or paragraphs reference the same source, without interruption by material citing a different source, note reference markers are generally placed at the end of those sequences in order to improve readability.

Chapter 1 Angels of Za'atari

1 Wafa T. Qusous & Kamil Adil, A Plane that Brings Love (2017).
2 Christa Case Bryant, *Syrian Refugees Top 2 Million – and Zaatari Camp Prepares for the Long Haul*, Christian Science Monitor (Sept. 4, 2013), www.csmonitor.com/World/Middle-East/2013/0903/Syrian-refugees-top-2-million-and-Zaatari-camp-prepares-for-long-haul; Amjad Tadros,

COVID Creeps into a Sprawling Syrian Refugee Camp in Jordan, CBS NEWS (Sept. 11, 2020), www.cbsnews.com/news/covid-cases-confirmed-in-sprawling-zaatari-syrian-refugee-camp-in-jordan.

Chapter 2 Olive Trees

1 Anthony Shadid, *Syria Escalates Crackdown as Tanks Go to Restive City,* NEW YORK TIMES (Apr. 25, 2011), www.nytimes .com/2011/04/26/world/middleeast/26syria.html.

2 Peter H. Gleik, *Water, Drought, Climate Change, and Conflict in Syria,* 6 WEATHER, CLIMATE, AND SOCIETY 331 (2014), https://journals.ametsoc.org/view/journals/wcas/6/3/wcas-d-13-00059_1.xml?tab_body=pdf; *How Could a Drought Spark a Civil War?,* NPR (Sept. 8, 2013), www.npr.org/2013/09/08/ 220438728/how-could-a-drought-spark-a-civil-war.

3 Hernando De Soto, *The Real Mohamed Bouazizi,* FOREIGN POLICY (Dec. 16, 2011), https://foreignpolicy.com/2011/12/16/ the-real-mohamed-bouazizi.

4 Thessa Lageman, *Mohamed Bouazizi: Was the Arab Spring Worth Dying For?,* AL JAZEERA (Jan. 3, 2016), www.aljazeera .com/news/2015/12/mohamed-bouazizi-arab-spring-worth-dying-151228093743375.html.

5 De Soto, *supra* note 3.

6 Lageman, *supra* note 4.

7 Id.

8 Id.

9 De Soto, *supra* note 3.

10 Lageman, *supra* note 4.

11 De Soto, *supra* note 3.

12 Angelique Chrisafis & Ian Black, *Zine al-Abidine Ben Ali Forced to Flee Tunisia as Protesters Claim Victory,* THE

GUARDIAN (Jan. 14, 2011), www.theguardian.com/world/2011/jan/14/tunisian-president-flees-country-protests.

13 Merrit Kennedy, *A Look at Egypt's Uprising, 5 Years Later*, NPR (Jan. 25, 2016), www.npr.org/sections/thetwo-way/2016/01/25/464290769/a-look-at-egypts-uprising-5-years-later.

14 Id.; *Egypt Unrest: 846 Killed in Protests – Official Toll*, BBC NEWS (Apr. 19, 2011), www.bbc.com/news/world-middle-east-13134956.

15 Jamie Tarabay, *For Many Syrians, the Story of the War Began with Graffiti in Dara'a*, CNN (Mar. 15, 2018), www.cnn.com/2018/03/15/middleeast/daraa-syria-seven-years-on-intl/index.html.

16 Id.

17 Zeina Karam, *In Ruins, Syria Marks 50 Years of Assad Family Rule*, AP NEWS (Nov. 12, 2020), https://apnews.com/article/iran-lebanon-france-bashar-assad-syria-ecb41dfa5da2938774 0a5fadaa27d31e.

18 Tarabay, *supra* note 15.

19 Id.; Hugh Macleod, *Inside Deraa*, AL JAZEERA (Apr. 19, 2011), www.aljazeera.com/features/2011/4/19/inside-deraa.

20 Sarah Dadouch, *Escalating Violence in Strategic Syrian City Belies Assad's Claim that He's In Control*, WASHINGTON POST (Nov. 24, 2020), www.washingtonpost.com/world/middle_east/assad-syria-daraa-violence/2020/11/23/28078628-243e-11eb-9c4a-0dc6242c4814_story.html; Yolande Knell, *Camp for Syrian Refugees Starts to Look More Like Home*, BBC NEWS (Mar. 14, 2014), www.bbc.com/news/world-middle-east-26565060.

21 Joe Sterling, *Daraa: The Spark that Lit the Syrian Flame*, CNN (Mar. 1, 2012), www.cnn.com/2012/03/01/world/meast/syria-crisis-beginnings/index.html.

22 James Snell, *Daraa Protests Show that City Remains outside Regime's Orbit*, ARAB WEEKLY (Mar. 17, 2019), https://thearabweekly.com/daraa-protests-show-city-remains-outside-regimes-orbit.

23 *Syria: The Story of the Conflict*, BBC NEWS (Mar. 11, 2016), www.bbc.com/news/world-middle-east-26116868; *Officers Fire on Crowd as Syrian Protests Grow*, NEW YORK TIMES (Mar. 20, 2011), www.nytimes.com/2011/03/21/world/middleeast/21syria.html.

24 Shadid, *supra* note 1.

25 Id.

26 Id.

27 Id.

28 *Syria Protests: Rights Group Warns of "Deraa Massacre,"* BBC NEWS (May 5, 2011), www.bbc.com/news/world-middle-east-13299793 (citing *Daraa: Ten Days of Massacres*, INTERNATIONAL FEDERATION FOR HUMAN RIGHTS (Apr. 5, 2011), www.fidh.org/en/region/north-africa-middle-east/syria/daraa-Ten-days-of-massacres).

29 Rick Gladstone & Hala Droubi, *New Rebel Gains Reported in Southern Syria with Seizure of Military Base*, NEW YORK TIMES (Apr. 3, 2013), www.nytimes.com/2013/04/04/world/middleeast/Syria-rebels.html.

30 Knell, *supra* note 20; Sybella Wilkes, *Jordan Opens New Camp for Syrian Refugees amid Funding Gaps*, UNCHR (July 30, 2012), www.unhcr.org/en-us/news/makingdifference/2012/7/5016861c9/jordan-opens-new-camp-syrian-refugees-amid-funding-gaps.html.

31 Affordable Housing Institute, ZAATARI: THE INSTANT CITY (2014), http://sigus.scripts.mit.edu/x/files/zaatari/AHIPublication.pdf; Jodi Rudoren, Lynsey Addario & Tamir Elterman, *Syrian Refugees Struggle at Zaatari*, NEW YORK TIMES (2013), http://archive.nytimes.com/www.nytimes.com/interactive/2013/05/09/world/middleeast/zaatari.html.

32 Peter Beaumont, *Jordan Opens New Syrian Refugee Camp*, THE GUARDIAN (Apr. 30, 2014), www.theguardian.com/world/2014/apr/30/jordan-new-syrian-refugee-camp-al-azraq.

33 Nikita Gill, "Home Was Your Refuge, Now They Call You Refugee." Poem provided at UNTAMED, UNWANTED PRETTY THINGS, https://untamedunwanted.tumblr.com/post/ 128991554148/home-is-a-language-you-grew-in-your-mouth-that.

34 Widad Nabi, "The Place Is Lit with Memory." Poem provided at *Poetry by Asma Jelassi and Widad Nabi, Translated from Arabic*, COLUMBIA JOURNAL (Aug. 28, 2018).

Chapter 3 Gray Walls

1 Justin Schon, *The Centrality of Checkpoints for Civilians during Conflict*, 18 CIVIL WARS 281 (2016), www.tandfonline.com/ doi/full/10.1080/13698249.2016.1215638.

2 Sybella Wilkes, *Jordan Opens New Camp for Syrian Refugees amid Funding Gaps*, UNCHR (July 30, 2012), www.unhcr.org/ en-us/news/makingdifference/2012/7/5016861c9/jordan-opens-new-camp-syrian-refugees-amid-funding-gaps.html.

3 Taylor Luck, *Protests Continue at Zaatari Camp as Community Leaders Emerge*, JORDAN TIMES (Nov. 5, 2012), https://web.archive.org/web/20121105202910/http://jordantimes .com/protests-continue-at-zaatari-camp-as-community-leaders-emerge.

4 *Syria Crisis: Deadly Clash in Jordan's Zaatari Camp*, BBC NEWS (Apr. 6, 2014), www.bbc.com/news/world-middle-east-26908587.

5 Author Interview with Rufut (June 2019) (audio on file with author).

6 UNICEF, SHATTERED LIVES: CHALLENGES AND PRIORITIES FOR SYRIAN CHILDREN AND WOMEN IN JORDAN (2013), https://reliefweb.int/sites/reliefweb.int/files/ resources/Shattered_Lives_June10.pdf; Affordable Housing Institute, ZAATARI: THE INSTANT CITY (2014), http://sigus .scripts.mit.edu/x/files/zaatari/AHIPublication.pdf.

7 Id.

8 Save the Children, TOO YOUNG TO WED: THE GROWING PROBLEM OF CHILD MARRIAGE AMONG SYRIAN GIRLS IN JORDAN (2014), https://jordan.savethechildren.net/sites/jordan .savethechildren.net/files/library/Too%20Young%20to% 20Wed%207th%20pp.pdf.

9 Id.

10 Lin Taylor, *Syrian Girls Flee War Only to Become Mothers in Jordan Camp*, REUTERS (Dec. 15, 2016), www.reuters.com/ article/us-jordan-refugees-childmarriage/syrian-girls-flee-war-only-to-become-mothers-in-jordan-camp-idUSKBN1441FO.

11 Save the Children, *supra* note 8.

12 Australian Aid, REMOVING BARRIERS: THE PATH TOWARD INCLUSIVE ACCESS (2018).

13 Id.

14 Id.

15 *Syrians with Mental, Physical Disabilities Face Greater Challenges as Refugees*, VOA NEWS (June 7, 2013). Video provided at: www.youtube.com/watch?v=nINqkCXBh_0.

16 Id.

17 Id.

18 Interview with Salma. Link to video no longer available.

19 Affordable Housing Institute, *supra* note 6.

Chapter 4 Global Crisis

1 Hannah Bloch, *That Little Syrian Boy: Here's Who He Was*, NPR (Sept. 3, 2015), www.npr.org/sections/parallels/2015/09/ 03/437132793/photo-of-dead-3-year-old-syrian-refugee-breaks-hearts-around-the-world.

2 Emina Osmandzikovic, *The Drowning of Aylan Kurdi*, ARAB NEWS (Apr. 18, 2020), www.arabnews.com/node/1660926.

3 Bryan Walsh, *Alan Kurdi's Story: Behind the Most Heartbreaking Photo of 2015*, TIME (Dec. 29, 2015), https://time.com/4162306/alan-kurdi-syria-drowned-boy-refugee-crisis.

4 Diane Cole, *Study: What Was the Impact of the Iconic Photo of the Syrian Boy?*, NPR (Jan. 13, 2017), www.npr.org/sections/goatsandsoda/2017/01/13/509650251/study-what-was-the-impact-of-the-iconic-photo-of-the-syrian-boy.

5 Ishaan Tharoor, *Death of Drowned Syrian Toddler Aylan Kurdi Jolts World Leaders*, WASHINGTON POST (Sept. 3, 2015), www.washingtonpost.com/news/worldviews/wp/2015/09/03/image-of-drowned-syrian-toddler-aylan-kurdi-jolts-world-leaders.

6 Laura Bush, *Separating Children from Their Parents at the Border "Breaks My Heart,"* WASHINGTON POST (June 17, 2018), www.washingtonpost.com/opinions/laura-bush-separating-children-from-their-parents-at-the-border-breaks-my-heart/2018/06/17/f2df517a-7287-11e8-9780-b1dd6a09b549_story.html; Jeh Charles Johnson, *Trump's "Zero-Tolerance" Border Policy Is Immoral, Un-American – and Ineffective*, WASHINGTON POST (June 18, 2018), www.washingtonpost.com/opinions/trumps-zero-tolerance-border-policy-is-immoral-un-american–and-ineffective/2018/06/18/efc4c514-732d-11e8-b4b7-308400242c2e_story.html.

7 Brian Naylor, *Fact Check: Trump Wrongly States Obama Administration Had Child Separation Policy*, NPR (Apr. 9, 2019), www.npr.org/2019/04/09/711446917/fact-check-trump-wrongly-states-obama-administration-had-child-separation-policy.

8 Molly Ball, *Trump Backed Down, But the Crisis at the Border Is Far from Over*, TIME (June 21, 2018), https://time.com/5318253/donald-trump-border-crisis-continues.

9 Sometimes "refugee crisis" is used to refer to a particular event in a part of the world (e.g., the Syrian refugee crisis). This discussion refers more broadly to the "global refugee crisis," or the sum of all the regional crises across the world. Sadly,

there are more refugees around the globe today than ever before, making today's global refugee crisis the largest in history. USA for UNHCR, *Refugee Statistics*, www.unrefugees.org/refugee-facts/statistics ("[T]he world's forcibly displaced population remained at a record high. This includes: 26.4 million refugees in the world – the highest ever seen …").

10 UNHCR, *Global Trends: Forced Displacement in 2020*, www.unhcr.org/flagship-reports/globaltrends.

11 *1 Per Cent of Humanity Displaced: UNHCR Global Trends Report*, UNHCR (June 18, 2020), www.unhcr.org/en-us/news/ press/2020/6/5ee9db2e4/1-cent-humanity-displaced-unhcr-global-trends-report.html.

12 Phillip Connor, *Nearly 1 in 100 Worldwide Are Now Displaced from Their Homes*, PEW RESEARCH (Aug. 3, 2016), www.pewresearch.org/fact-tank/2016/10/05/key-facts-about-the-worlds-refugees.

13 UNHCR, ZA'ATARI CAMP FACT SHEET (June 2021), https://reliefweb.int/report/jordan/unhcr-jordan-zaatari-refugee-camp-factsheet-june-2021.

14 *Global Trends, supra* note 10.

15 UNHCR, *Children*, www.unhcr.org/en-us/children-49c3646c1e8.html.

16 Council on Foreign Relations, NO REFUGE: WHY THE WORLD'S SWELLING REFUGEE POPULATION HAS SHRINKING OPTIONS, www.cfr.org/interactive/refugee-crisis/ #!/a-system-under-strain.

17 Note, *American Courts and the U.N. High Commissioner for Refugees: A Need for Harmony in the Face of a Refugee Crisis*, 131 HARVARD LAW REVIEW 1399 (2018), https:// harvardlawreview.org/2018/03/american-courts-and-the-u-n-high-commissioner-for-refugees-a-need-for-harmony-in-the-face-of-a-refugee-crisis; *Global Trends, supra* note 10.

18 *Global Trends, supra* note 10 ("During 2020, several crises – some new, some longstanding and some resurfacing after years – forced 11.2 million people to flee . . .").

19 Id.

20 Kathryn Reid, *Forced to Flee: Top Countries Refugees Are Coming From*, WORLD VISION (June 18, 2021), www.worldvision.org/refugees-news-stories/forced-to-flee-top-countries-refugees-coming-from; *Global Trends, supra* note 10.

21 UNHCR, *Refugee Data Finder* (Dec. 8, 2020), www.unhcr.org/refugee-statistics.

22 *Syria Conflict at 5 Years: The Biggest Refugee and Displacement Crisis of Our Time Demands a Huge Surge in Solidarity*, UNHCR (Mar. 15, 2016), https://www.unhcr.org/en-us/news/press/2016/3/56e6e3249/syria-conflict-5-years-biggest-refugee-displacement-crisis-time-demands.html (quoting the UN High Commissioner for Refugees, Filippo Grandi, in stating, "Syria is the biggest humanitarian and refugee crisis of our time, a continuing cause of suffering for millions which should be garnering a groundswell of support around the world.").

23 Council on Foreign Relations, *Civil War in Syria* (Sept. 8, 2021), www.cfr.org/global-conflict-tracker/conflict/civil-war-syria; U.S. Institute of Peace, *The Current Situation in Syria: A USIP Fact Sheet* (Aug. 26, 2020), www.usip.org/publications/2020/08/current-situation-syria.

24 Human Rights Watch, WORLD REPORT 2021 (2021), www.hrw.org/world-report/2021/country-chapters/syria.

25 Zachary Laub, *Syria's Civil War: The Descent into Horror*, COUNCIL ON FOREIGN RELATIONS (Mar. 17, 2021), www.cfr.org/article/syrias-civil-war.

26 *Refugee Statistics, supra* note 9; U.S. Census Bureau, *City and Town Population Totals: 2010-2019*, www.census.gov/data/datasets/time-series/demo/popest/2010s-total-cities-and-towns.html

(the population of New York City in 2019 was 8.337 million, and the population of Los Angeles was 3.980 million. The sum, 12.317 million, is lower than the estimated 13.5 million Syrians displaced since the war began).

27 *Refugee Statistics, supra* note 9.

28 Kathryn Reid, *Syrian Refugee Crisis: Facts, FAQs, and How to Help*, WORLD VISION (July 13, 2021), www.worldvision.org/ refugees-news-stories/syrian-refugee-crisis-facts; UNICEF USA, *How to Help Syrian Children*, www.unicefusa.org/ mission/emergencies/child-refugees-and-migrants/syria-crisis.

29 *The Current Situation in Syria, supra* note 23.

30 *Syria War: "World Shrugs" as 103 Civilians Killed in 10 Days*, BBC NEWS (July 26, 2019), www.bbc.com/news/world-middle-east-49126523.

31 Human Rights Watch, *supra* note 24; Human Rights Watch, WORLD REPORT 2020 (2020), www.hrw.org/world-report/2020/country-chapters/syria.

32 *"I Would Rather Die Than Go Back": Rohingya Refugees Settle into Life in Bangladesh*, NPR (Aug. 24, 2018), www.npr.org/transcripts/641239849.

33 *Myanmar Rohingya: What You Need to Know about the Crisis*, BBC NEWS (Jan. 23, 2020), www.bbc.com/news/world-asia-41566561.

34 *Rohingya Crisis: Refugees Tell of "House by House" Killings*, BBC NEWS (Oct. 18, 2017), www.bbc.com/news/av/world-asia-41674965.

35 *Myanmar Rohingya, supra* note 33.

36 Human Rights Council, REPORT OF THE INDEPENDENT INTERNATIONAL FACT-FINDING MISSION ON MYANMAR (Sept. 2018); Jason Beaubien, *In Bangladeshi Camps, Rohingya Refugees Try to Move Forward with Their Lives*, NPR (Aug. 30, 2018), www.npr.org/2018/08/30/643008438/in-bangladeshi-

camps-rohingya-refugees-try-to-move-forward-with-their-lives.

37 *Myanmar's Genocide against Rohingya Not Over, Says Rights Group*, THE GUARDIAN (Nov. 23, 2020), www.theguardian .com/world/2020/nov/23/myanmar-is-still-committing-genocide-against-rohingya-says-rights-group.

38 Rocio Cara Labrador & Danielle Renwick, *Central America's Violent Northern Triangle*, COUNCIL ON FOREIGN RELATIONS (June 26, 2018), www.cfr.org/backgrounder/ central-americas-violent-northern-triangle. Part of this section on refugees and asylum seekers from the Northern Triangle of Central America is adapted from the author's work in the *Harvard Civil Rights-Civil Liberties Law Review*, which argues that there is a constitutional right to appointed counsel for children facing deportation in the US. Andrew Leon Hanna, Note, *A Constitutional Right to Appointed Counsel for the Children of America's Refugee Crisis*, 54 HARVARD CIVIL RIGHTS-CIVIL LIBERTIES LAW REVIEW 257 (2019).

39 World Bank, CRIME AND VIOLENCE IN CENTRAL AMERICA: A DEVELOPMENT CHALLENGE (2011), https://siteresources.worldbank.org/INTLAC/Resources/ FINAL_VOLUME_I_ENGLISH_CrimeAndViolence.pdf.

40 UNHCR, CENTRAL AMERICA REFUGEE CRISIS, www.unrefugees.org/emergencies/central-america.

41 Maureen Meyer & Elyssa Pachico, *Fact Sheet: U.S. Immigration and Central American Asylum Seekers*, WOLA (Feb. 1, 2018), www.wola.org/analysis/fact-sheet-united-states-immigration-central-american-asylum-seekers.

42 UNHCR, WOMEN ON THE RUN: FIRST-HAND ACCOUNTS OF REFUGEES FLEEING EL SALVADOR, GUATEMALA, HONDURAS, AND MEXICO (2015), www.unhcr.org/en-us/ publications/operations/5630f24c6/women-run.html.

43 Council on Foreign Relations, *supra* note 16; Reid, *supra* note 20; *Venezuela Crisis: How the Political Situation Escalated*, BBC News (Dec. 3, 2020), www.bbc.com/news/world-latin-america-36319877.

44 *Refugee Data Finder, supra* note 21.

45 Joseph Krauss, *Taliban Take Over Afghanistan: What We Know and What's Next*, AP News (Aug. 17, 2021), https://apnews.com/article/taliban-takeover-afghanistan-what-to-know-1a74c9cd866866f196c478aba21b60b6; *Afghanistan: Where Will Refugees Go after Taliban Takeover?*, BBC News (Aug. 28, 2021), www.bbc.com/news/world-asia-58283177.

46 *Yemen Crisis: Why Is There War?*, BBC News (June 19, 2020), www.bbc.com/news/world-middle-east-29319423; United Nations Relief and Works Agency for Palestine Refugees in the Near East, *Palestinian Refugees*, www.unrwa.org/palestine-refugees.

47 Lindsay Maizland, *China's Repression of Uyghurs in Xinjiang*, Council on Foreign Relations (Mar. 1, 2021), www.cfr.org/backgrounder/chinas-repression-uyghurs-xinjiang; *Uighurs: Western Countries Sanction China over Rights Abuses*, BBC News (Mar. 22, 2021), www.bbc.com/news/world-europe-56487162.

48 Kaamil Ahmed, *South Sudan Faces "Catastrophic" Famine unless Conflict Ended*, The Guardian (Dec. 18, 2020), www.theguardian.com/global-development/2020/dec/18/south-sudan-faces-catastrophic-famine-unless-conflict-ended; Joshua Keating, *Catastrophic Droughts Are Becoming the New Normal in Somalia*, Slate (Aug. 7, 2019), https://slate.com/news-and-politics/2019/08/somalia-drought-the-world-is-struggling-to-keep-up-with-climate-change-in-the-horn-of-africa.html; Ban Ki-Moon, *Famine in Somalia*, UN, www.un.org/africarenewal/web-features/famine-somalia; *Two Million People at Risk of Starvation as Drought Returns to*

Somalia, THE GUARDIAN (June 6, 2019), www.theguardian
.com/global-development/2019/jun/06/two-million-people-at-
risk-of-starvation-as-drought-returns-to-somalia; Robert
Muggah, *The U.N. Can't Bring Peace to the Central African
Republic*, FOREIGN POLICY (Aug. 16, 2018), https://
foreignpolicy.com/2018/08/16/the-u-n-cant-bring-peace-to-
the-central-african-republic; Reid, *supra* note 20.

49 Jean B. Nachega, Placide Mbala-Kingebeni, John Otshudiema,
Alimuddin Zumla & Jean-Jacques Muyembe Tam-Fum, *The
Colliding Epidemics of COVID-19, Ebola, and Measles in the
Democratic Republic of the Congo*, 8 THE LANCET 991 (June
23, 2020), www.thelancet.com/journals/langlo/article/PIIS2214-
109X(20)30281-3/fulltext; Henry Wilkins, *More than 160 Killed
in Deadliest Attack of Burkina Faso's War*, VOA NEWS (June
6, 2021), www.voanews.com/africa/more-160-killed-deadliest-
attack-burkina-fasos-war; *Record Numbers Forced to Flee
Ongoing Violence in Burkina Faso*, UNHCR (July 23, 2021),
www.unhcr.org/en-us/news/briefing/2021/7/60fa77864/record-
numbers-forced-flee-ongoing-violence-burkina-faso.html;
DR Congo Tops List of World's Most Neglected Crises,
NORWEGIAN REFUGEE COUNCIL (May 26, 2021),
www.nrc.no/news/2021/may/dr-congo-tops-list-of-worlds-
most-neglected-crises; *Burkina Faso's War against Militant
Islamists*, BBC NEWS (May 30, 2019), www.bbc.com/news/
world-africa-39279050.

50 *Refugee Camps*, UNHCR, www.unrefugees.org/refugee-facts/
camps.

51 Simon Turner, *What Is a Refugee Camp?: Explorations of the
Limits and Effects of the Camp*, 29 JOURNAL OF REFUGEE
STUDIES 139 (Dec. 31, 2015), https://academic.oup.com/jrs/
article-abstract/29/2/139/2362940?redirectedFrom=fulltext.

52 *Rohingya Crisis: A Firsthand Look into the World's Largest
Refugee Camp*, UN WORLD FOOD PROGRAM USA (Dec. 8,

2020), www.wfpusa.org/articles/rohingya-crisis-a-firsthand-look-into-the-worlds-largest-refugee-camp.

53 *UN Teams Assisting Tens of Thousands of Refugees, after Massive Fire Rips through Camp in Bangladesh*, UN News (Mar. 23, 2021), https://news.un.org/en/story/2021/03/1088012.

54 *Rohingya River Crossing*, Reuters (Dec. 27, 2017), www.reuters.com/news/picture/rohingya-river-crossing-idUSRTS1I1SO.

55 UNA-USA, *Dadaab Refugee Camp*, https://unausa.org/adopt-a-future/dadaab.

56 Ki-Moon, *supra* note 48.

57 Daniel Wesangula, *Rights Groups Welcome Court Ruling to Block Kenya Refugee Camp Closure*, The Guardian (Feb. 9, 2017), www.theguardian.com/world/2017/feb/09/kenyan-court-quashes-government-order-close-refugee-camp.

58 UNHCR, *Dadaab Refugee Complex*, www.unhcr.org/ke/dadaab-refugee-complex.

59 *Life in Limbo: Inside the World's 10 Largest Refugee Camps*, ESRI, https://storymaps.esri.com/stories/2016/refugee-camps.

60 Mohamad Alloush, J. Edward Tayloe, Anubhab Gupta, Ruben Irvin Rojas Valders & Ernesto Gonzalez-Estrada, *Economic Life in Refugee Camps*, 95 World Development 334 (2017); Unite for Sight, *Module 3: Food, Water, Sanitation, and Housing in Refugee Camps*, www.uniteforsight.org/refugee-health/module3.

61 Marissa Taylor, *9 Facts about the Refugee Water Crisis*, Borgen Project (Mar. 18, 2020), https://borgenproject.org/refugee-water-crisis.

62 Unite for Sight, *Module 1: Healthcare in Refugee Camps and Settlements*, www.uniteforsight.org/refugee-health/module1.

63 *More than Half of World's Refugee Children "Do Not Get an Education," Warns UNHCR*, UN News (Aug. 30, 2019),

https://news.un.org/en/story/2019/08/1045281; Unite for Sight, *Module 4: Children and Education in Refugee Camps*, www.uniteforsight.org/refugee-health/module4.

64 *Module 3*, *supra* note 60; *UN Targets Electrifying All of World's Refugee Camps*, FRANCE24 (Dec. 19, 2019), www.france24 .com/en/20191219-un-targets-electrifying-all-of-world-s-refugee-camps.

65 Unite for Sight, *Module 5: Refugee Camp Economies*, www.uniteforsight.org/refugee-health/module5.

66 *Jordan's First Job Centre for Syrian Refugees Opens in Zaatari Camp*, INTERNATIONAL LABOUR ORGANIZATION (Aug. 21, 2017), www.ilo.org/beirut/media-centre/news/WCMS_570884/ lang–en/index.htm.

67 Lauren Parater, *10 Refugees Who Will Change Your Perception of Entrepreneurship*, UNHCR (June 5, 2016), www.unhcr.org/ innovation/10-refugees-who-will-change-your-perception-of-entrepreneurship; Urvashi Sarkar, *With No Formal Schools or Jobs, Young Rohingya Left in Lurch*, AL JAZEERA (Apr. 13, 2018), www.aljazeera.com/features/2018/4/13/with-no-formal-schools-or-jobs-young-rohingya-left-in-lurch; Nina Strochlic, *In Uganda, a Unique Urban Experiment Is Under Way*, NATIONAL GEOGRAPHIC (Apr. 2019), www.nationalgeographic.com/magazine/2019/04/how-bidibidi-uganda-refugee-camp-became-city; *Module 5*, *supra* note 65.

68 Alloush, Tayloe, Gupta, Valders & Gonzalez-Estrada, *supra* note 60; Rahul Oka, *Unlikely Cities in the Desert: The Informal Economy as Causal Agent for Permanent "Urban" Sustainability in Kakuma Refugee Camp, Kenya*, 40 URBAN ANTHROPOLOGY AND STUDIES OF CULTURAL SYSTEMS AND WORLD ECONOMIC DEVELOPMENT 223 (2011), www.jstor.org/stable/23339794.

69 *Refugee Camps*, *supra* note 50.

70 Amnesty International, *The World's Refugees in Numbers*, www.amnesty.org/en/what-we-do/refugees-asylum-seekers-and-migrants/global-refugee-crisis-statistics-and-facts.

71 *UN Refugee Chief Laments Nearly 90 Million People Forcibly Displaced*, UN NEWS (June 18, 2020), https://news.un.org/en/story/2020/06/1066492.

72 Zoe Todd, *By the Numbers: Syrian Refugees around the World*, PBS (Nov. 19, 2019), www.pbs.org/wgbh/frontline/article/numbers-syrian-refugees-around-world; World Bank, *World Bank Country and Lending Groups* (2020), https://datahelpdesk.worldbank.org/knowledgebase/articles/906519-world-bank-country-and-lending-groups (country classifications by income).

73 Vicky Kelberer, *Putting Refugee Work Permits to Work*, 278 MIDDLE EAST REPORT 16 (2016), https://merip.org/2016/04/putting-refugee-work-permits-to-work.

74 Helen Dempster, Thomas Ginn, Jimmy Graham, Martha Guerrero Ble, Daphne Jayasinghe & Barri Shorey, *Locked Down and Left Behind: The Impact of COVID-19 on Refugees' Economic Inclusion*, REFUGEES INTERNATIONAL (July 8, 2020), www.refugeesinternational.org/reports/2020/7/6/locked-down-and-left-behind-the-impact-of-covid-19-on-refugees-economic-inclusion.

75 COUNCIL ON FOREIGN RELATIONS, *supra* note 16.

76 Convention Relating to the Status of Refugees, July 28, 1951, 19 U.S.T. 6259, 189 U.N.T.S. 150; Protocol Relating to the Status of Refugees, Jan. 31, 1967, 19 U.S.T. 6223, 606 U.N.T.S. 267; *American Courts and the U.N. High Commissioner for Refugees*, *supra* note 17.

77 Id.

78 UNHCR, *Refugees in America*, www.unrefugees.org/refugee-facts/usa.

79 *Refugee Resettlement: "Tremendous Gap" Persists between Needs, and Spaces on Offer*, UN NEWS (Feb. 5, 2020), https://news.un.org/en/story/2020/02/1056742.

80 *Refugees in America, supra* note 78.

81 Harvard Law School – Harvard Immigration and Refugee Clinical Program, FULFILLING U.S. COMMITMENT TO REFUGEE RESETTLEMENT: PROTECTING REFUGEES, PRESERVING NATIONAL SECURITY & BUILDING THE U.S. ECONOMY THROUGH REFUGEE ADMISSIONS (May 2017), https://harvardimmigrationclinic.files.wordpress.com/2017/06/syria-final-draft-v9.pdf; U.S. State Department, *Refugee Admissions*, www.state.gov/j/prm/ra; *Refugees in America, supra* note 78.

82 *U.S. Resettles Fewer Refugees, Even as Global Number of Displaced People Grows*, PEW RESEARCH CENTER (Oct. 12, 2017), www.pewresearch.org/global/2017/10/12/u s resettles-fewer-refugees-even-as-global-number-of-displaced-people-grows/#fn-39130-2.

83 Emma Lazarus, "The New Colossus." Poem provided at *Statute of Liberty*, NATIONAL PARK SERVICE, www.nps.gov/stli/learn/historyculture/colossus.htm.

84 John Campbell, *U.S. Refugee Resettlement Shrinking as Need from Africa Continues to Grow*, COUNCIL ON FOREIGN RELATIONS (Aug. 8, 2019), www.cfr.org/blog/us-refugee-resettlement-shrinking-need-africa-continues-growing.

85 National Immigration Forum, *Fact Sheet: U.S. Refugee Resettlement* (Nov. 5, 2020), https://immigrationforum.org/article/fact-sheet-u-s-refugee-resettlement.

86 Saliho Touré, *Like Syrians Now, My Family Fled Liberia as Refugees. Unlike Syrians, America Welcomed Us*, USA TODAY (Sept. 4, 2019), www.usatoday.com/story/opinion/voices/2019/09/04/syria-civil-war-liberia-refugees-program-trump-cuts-column/2196996001; Katie Zezima, *The U.S. Has Slashed Its*

Refugee Intake. Syrians Fleeing War Are Most Affected, WASHINGTON POST (May 7, 2019), www.washingtonpost .com/immigration/the-us-has-slashed-its-refugee-intake-syrians-fleeing-war-are-most-affected/2019/05/07/f764e57c-678f-11e9-a1b6-b29b90efa879_story.html.

87 *COVID-19 Crisis Underlines Need for Refugee Solidarity and Inclusion*, UNHCR (Oct. 7, 2020), www.unhcr.org/en-us/news/ latest/2020/10/5f7dfbc24/covid-19-crisis-underlines-need-refugee-solidarity-inclusion.html.

88 *UNHCR Warns 2020 Risks Lowest Resettlement Levels in Recent History*, UNHCR (Nov. 19, 2020), www.unhcr.org/en-us/news/ press/2020/11/5fb4e6f24/unhcr-warns-2020-risks-lowest-resettlement-levels-recent-history.html.

89 Council on Foreign Relations, *supra* note 16.

90 Campbell, *supra* note 84.

Chapter 5 New Beginnings

1 Interview with Malak, RADIO LEQAA FM (2019). Video provided at: www.facebook.com/watch/live/?v= 401113853954855&ref=watch_permalink.

2 Id.

3 Phil Knight, SHOE DOG: A MEMOIR BY THE CREATOR OF NIKE (2016).

4 Conan O'Brien, Commencement Speech at Dartmouth College, TEAM COCO (2011). Video provided at: www.youtube .com/watch?v=KmDYXaaT9sA ("It's not easy, but if you accept your misfortune and handle it right, your perceived failure can become a catalyst for profound reinvention.").

5 Interview with Steve Jobs, COMPUTERWORLD INFORMATION TECHNOLOGY AWARDS FOUNDATION (1995). Video provided at: https://vimeo.com/31813340.

6 Martin Luther King, Jr., "I've Been to the Mountaintop" (Apr. 3, 1968). Speech transcript provided at: Nikita Stewart, *"I've Been to the Mountaintop," Dr. King's Last Sermon Annotated*, NEW YORK TIMES (Apr. 2, 2018), www.nytimes.com/interactive/2018/04/02/us/king-mlk-last-sermon-annotated.html.

7 Amineh Abou Kerech, "Lament for Syria." Poem provided at Killian Fox, *The 13-Year-Old Syrian Refugee Who Became a Prizewinning Poet*, THE GUARDIAN (Oct. 1, 2017), www.theguardian.com/books/2017/oct/01/the-13-year-old-syrian-refugee-prizewinning-poet-amineh-abou-kerech-betjeman-prize.

Chapter 6 Khatwa, Khatwa

1 Louay Constant, Shanthi Nataraj & Fadia Afashe, *As Refugees, Syrian Women Find Liberation in Working*, RAND (Feb. 19, 2019), www.rand.org/blog/2019/02/as-refugees-syrian-women-find-liberation-in-working.html; Lian Saifi, *Empowerment through Employment*, NORWEGIAN REFUGEE COUNCIL (Sept. 11, 2017), www.nrc.no/news/2017/september/empowerment-through-employment.

2 *DAFI Tertiary Scholarship Programme*, UNHCR, www.unhcr.org/en-us/dafi-scholarships.html.

3 Author Interview with Malwa (June 2019) (audio on file with author).

4 Interview with Eman, Save the Children Jordan (April 2019) (video interview provided by Save the Children Jordan; on file with author).

5 Id.

6 Id.

Chapter 7 Balloons

1 *Analysis: Politics and Power in Jordan's Za'atari Refugee Camp*, RELIEFWEB (Nov. 1, 2013), https://reliefweb.int/report/jordan/analysis-politics-and-power-jordans-zaatari-refugee-camp.

Chapter 8 Extreme Entrepreneurs

1 Lauren Parater, *10 Refugees Who Will Change Your Perception of Entrepreneurship*, UNHCR (June 5, 2016), www.unhcr.org/innovation/10-refugees-who-will-change-your-perception-of-entrepreneurship; Urvashi Sarkar, *With No Formal Schools or Jobs, Young Rohingya Left in Lurch*, AL JAZEERA (Apr. 13, 2018), www.aljazeera.com/features/2018/4/13/with-no-formal-schools-or-jobs-young-rohingya-left-in-lurch; Nina Strochlic, *In Uganda, a Unique Urban Experiment Is Under Way*, NATIONAL GEOGRAPHIC (Apr. 2019), www.nationalgeographic.com/magazine/2019/04/how-bidibidi-uganda-refugee-camp-became-city; *Module 5: Refugee Camp Economies*, UNITE FOR SIGHT, www.uniteforsight.org/refugee-health/module5.

2 Author Interview with Balighah (Dec. 2018) (audio on file with author).

3 Veronica Villafane, *Latino, Black and Middle-Eastern Immigrants Portrayed as Criminals on TV*, FORBES (May 18, 2017), www.forbes.com/sites/veronicavillafane/2017/05/18/latino-black-and-middle-eastern-immigrants-portrayed-as-criminals-on-hollywood-tv/?sh=3dff974417b6 (citing Opportunity Agenda, POWER OF POP (2017), www.opportunityagenda.org/explore/resources-publications/power-pop).

4 New American Economy, FROM STRUGGLE TO RESILIENCE (2017), www.newamericaneconomy.org/issues/refugees.

5 *Refugees Are the Most Entrepreneurial Migrants in Australia*, REFUGEE COUNCIL OF AUSTRALIA (Apr. 15, 2019), www.refugeecouncil.org.au/refugees-are-entrepreneurial.

6 *Investing in Refugee Entrepreneurship*, FOX BUSINESS (June 21, 2018). Video provided at: www.youtube.com/watch?v=vzP3BN9VfmU.

7 UNCHR, *Sherkole Refugee Camp* (Jan. 2018), https://data2.unhcr.org/en/documents/details/62699.

8 Emebet Abdissa, *Masika's New Future*, NORWEGIAN REFUGEE COUNCIL (Aug. 26, 2015), www.nrc.no/news/2015/august/masikas-new-future-/?categoryId=53; Andy Needham, *International Women's Day 2015: Former Kinshasa Cabbie Earns a Crust Feeding Refugees and Aid Workers*, UNHCR (Mar. 6, 2015), www.unhcr.org/en-us/news/latest/2015/3/54f9cc876/international-womens-day-2015-former-kinshasa-cabbie-earns-crust-feeding.html.

9 Needham, *supra* note 8.

10 Abdissa, *supra* note 8.

11 Needham, *supra* note 8.

12 Abdissa, *supra* note 8.

13 Id.

14 Peter Vandor & Nikolaus Franke, *Why Are Immigrants More Entrepreneurial?*, HARVARD BUSINESS REVIEW (Oct. 27, 2016), https://hbr.org/2016/10/why-are-immigrants-more-entrepreneurial.

15 U.K. Department for Work and Pensions, *How Razan Became an Award-Winning Business Woman with New Enterprise Allowance* (Aug. 21, 2017). Video provided at: www.youtube.com/watch?v=CH7EPwFqugo.

16 Id.

17 *Refugee's Success as Producer of Middle Eastern Cheese*, AP NEWS (May 1, 2017). Video provided at: www.youtubc.com/watch?v=b1gyQMUokHo.

18 Anna Pukas, *Meet the Cheese Maker with a Lot of Bottle*, ARAB NEWS (Aug. 20, 2018), www.arabnews.com/node/1358196/food-health; Matt Smith, *The UK Must Embrace Refugees' Entrepreneurial Potential*, HUFFINGTON POST (June 4, 2018), www.huffingtonpost.co.uk/entry/the-uk-must-embrace-refugees-entrepreneurial-potential_uk_5ac5f500e4b01f556d5 658ca.

19 Pukas, *supra* note 18.

20 Abhijit Mohanty, *How Refugees in Ghana and Liberia Started a School for Their Own*, THE WIRE (Dec. 5, 2017), https://thewire .in/external-affairs/refugees-ghana-liberia-children-schools.

21 Jackie Edwards, *Africa's Refugee-Camp Entrepreneurs*, OPEN POLITICAL ECONOMY NETWORK (June 2, 2017), www.opennetwork.net/africas-refugee-camp-entrepreneurs; Hannah Garrard, *Of Book Thieves and Bribery*, NEW INTERNATIONALIST (June 18, 2014), https://newint.org/blog/ 2014/06/18/book-thieves-bribery-liberia; Mohanty, *supra* note 20.

22 Mohanty, *supra* note 20.

23 *Software Pioneer and Philanthropist Dame Stephanie Shirley*, FINANCIAL TIMES (Mar. 13, 2015), www.ft.com/content/ f8a48686-c32e-11e4-9c27-00144feab7de; *Dame Stephanie "Steve" Shirley*, UNITED NATIONS SYSTEM STAFF COLLEGE, www.unssc.org/about-unssc/speakers-and-collaborators/ dame-stephanie-steve-shirley.

24 Id. (citing Dame Stephanie Shirley & Richard Askwith, LET IT GO (2012)).

25 Stephen Beard, *Why Refugees Make Great Entrepreneurs*, MARKETPLACE (Aug. 7, 2019), www.marketplace.org/2019/08/ 07/why-refugees-make-great-entrepreneurs.

26 Id.

27 Author Interview with Chip (Dec. 2018) (audio on file with author).

28 Dina Gerdeman, *Minorities Who 'Whiten' Job Resumes Get More Interviews*, HARVARD BUSINESS SCHOOL (May 17, 2017), https://hbswk.hbs.edu/item/minorities-who-whiten-job-resumes-get-more-interviews (citing Sonia K. Kang, Katherine A. DeCelles, András Tilcsik & Sora Jun, *Whitened Résumés: Race and Self-Presentation in the Labor Market*, 61 ADMINISTRATIVE SCIENCE QUARTERLY 469 (2016), https://journals.sagepub.com/doi/abs/10.1177/0001839216639577).

29 Daniel Widner & Stephen Chicoine, *It's All in the Name: Employment Discrimination against Arab Americans*, 26 EASTERN SOCIOLOGICAL SOCIETY 806 (2011), www.jstor.org/stable/41330896?seq=1#page_scan_tab_contents.

30 German Lopez, *Study: Anti-Black Hiring Discrimination Is as Prevalent Today as It Was in 1989*, VOX (Sept. 18, 2017), www.vox.com/identities/2017/9/18/16307782/study-racism-jobs (citing Lincoln Quillian, Devah Pager, Ole Hexel & Arnfinn H. Midtbøen, *Meta-Analysis of Field Experiments Shows No Change in Racial Discrimination in Hiring over Time*, 114 PROCEEDINGS OF THE NATIONAL ACADEMY OF SCIENCES 10870 (2017), www.pnas.org/content/114/41/10870.full).

31 Vandor & Franke, *supra* note 14.

32 Linda Rabben, *Credential Recognition for Foreign Professionals in the United States*, MIGRATION POLICY INSTITUTE (2013), www.migrationpolicy.org/pubs/UScredentialrecognition.pdf.

33 Alfred Lubrano, *Brain Waste: Immigrants with Foreign Degrees Find U.S. Employers Reluctant to Hire Them*, THE INQUIRER (Apr. 6, 2018), www.philly.com/philly/news/brain-waste-immigrants-foreign-college-degrees-philly-mal-employment-20180406.html.

34 *NJPP: Immigrant Small Business Ownership Is a Cornerstone of New Jersey's Economy*, INSIDERNJ (Mar. 18, 2019), www.insidernj.com/press-release/njpp-immigrant-small-

business-ownership-cornerstone-new-jerseys-economy
(quoting Carlos Medina of the Statewide Hispanic Chamber of
Commerce of New Jersey, who observes that many of the
state's businesses are "started by immigrants that come to this
country overqualified for the jobs they are offered and prefer to
take their skills and become entrepreneurs").

35 Beard, *supra* note 25.

36 Id.

37 Abdissa, *supra* note 8.

38 Anna Zacharias, *"Work Is Life" for the Refugee-Entrepreneurs
of Greece's Ritsona Camp*, THE NATIONAL (Oct. 14, 2018),
www.thenationalnews.com/uae/work-is-life-for-the-refugee-
entrepreneurs-of-greece-s-ritsona-camp-1.780386.

39 *How Razan Became an Award-Winning Business Woman with
New Enterprise Allowance*, *supra* note 15.

Chapter 9 Midnight Blue

1 *World's Largest Syrian Refugee Camp Has Developed Its Own
Economy*, PBS NEWSHOUR (June 18, 2016), www.pbs.org/
newshour/show/worlds-largest-syrian-refugee-camp-has-
developed-its-own-economy.

2 Azrin Rahman, *11 Brilliant Startup Accelerators and Incubators
for Migrant Entrepreneurs to Kick-Start*, STARTUPS
WITHOUT BORDERS (Dec. 11, 2018), https://startupswb.com/
blog/2018/12/11/11-brilliant-startup-accelerators-and-
incubators-for-migrant-entrepreneurs.

3 Id.

4 Christy Un & Lilly Carlisle, *Growing a Sustainable Community*,
UNCHR (Nov. 3, 2019), www.unhcr.org/jo/12200-growing-a-
sustainable-community.html; *Jordan Switches On World's
Largest Solar Plant in Refugee Camp*, REUTERS (Nov. 13, 2017),
www.reuters.com/article/us-jordan-solar-zaatari/jordan-

switches-on-worlds-largest-solar-plant-in-refugee-camp-idUSKBN1DD22N; *Iris Scan Helps Syrian Refugees in Jordan Receive UN Supplies in "Blink of an Eye,"* UN NEWS (Oct. 6, 2016), https://news.un.org/en/story/2016/10/542032-iris-scan-helps-syrian-refugees-jordan-receive-un-supplies-blink-eye.

5 Heather Stephenson, *Teaching Science – and Hope – in a Refugee Camp*, TUFTS NOW (July 5, 2018), https://now.tufts.edu/articles/teaching-science-and-hope-syrian-refugee-camp.

6 Email to author from Ayman Halaseh, STEM Design Squad (Dec. 6, 2018) (email on file with author).

7 Id.

8 Stephenson, *supra* note 5.

9 *Refugee with Disability Overcomes Steep Hurdles*, UNFPA (July 27, 2015), www.unfpa.org/news/refugee-disability-overcomes-steep-hurdles.

10 Id.

11 Id.

12 Interview with Malak, RADIO LEQAA FM (2019). Video provided at: www.facebook.com/watch/live/?v=401113853954855&ref=watch_permalink.

13 Save the Children, TOO YOUNG TO WED: THE GROWING PROBLEM OF CHILD MARRIAGE AMONG SYRIAN GIRLS IN JORDAN (2014), https://jordan.savethechildren.net/sites/jordan.savethechildren.net/files/library/Too%20Young%20to%20Wed%207th%20pp.pdf.

14 Id.

Chapter 10 Dignity

1 Interview with Malak, RADIO LEQAA FM (2019). Video provided at: www.facebook.com/watch/live/?v=401113853954855&ref=watch_permalink.

Chapter 11 Global Catalyst

1 Sara Abdel-Rahim, *In a Refugee Camp, Entrepreneurship Thrives in Isobox Containers*, MEDIUM (Feb. 1, 2018), https:// medium.com/athenslivegr/in-a-refugee-camp-entrepreneurship-thrives-in-isobox-containers-115d6e9833e9.

2 Nina Strochlic, *In Uganda, a Unique Urban Experiment Is Under Way*, NATIONAL GEOGRAPHIC (Apr. 2019), www.nationalgeographic.com/magazine/2019/04/how-bidibidi-uganda-refugee-camp-became-city.

3 UNHCR, DOING BUSINESS IN DADAAB (2019), https:// reliefweb.int/sites/reliefweb.int/files/resources/Doing-Business-in-Dadaab-April-2019_Final-Report.pdf; Jackie Edwards, *Africa's Refugee-Camp Entrepreneurs*, OPEN POLITICAL ECONOMY NETWORK (June 2, 2017), www.opennetwork.net/ africas-refugee-camp-entrepreneurs.

4 *The Refugee Camp That Became a City*, UN, www.un.org/ africarenewal/news/refugee-camp-became-city.

5 Verena Hölzl, *Start-Up: The Rohingya Entrepreneurs Eking Out a Living in Refugee Camps*, NEW HUMANITARIAN (Apr. 29, 2019), www.thenewhumanitarian.org/feature/2019/04/29/Bangladesh-rohingya-entrepreneurs-eking-out-living-refugee-camps.

6 Matthew La Corte, *Refugees Are Revitalizing Some Great American Cities Facing Decline*, NISKANEN CENTER (June 21, 2016), www.niskanencenter.org/refugees-revitalizing-great-american-cities-facing-decline.

7 Id.

8 *What Happened When This Struggling City Opened Its Arms to Refugees*, PBS NEWSHOUR (July 6, 2017), www.pbs.org/ newshour/show/happened-struggling-city-opened-arms-refugees. The discussions about Utica, New York, in this book benefited greatly from the author's interviews with several local and regional community leaders, including: Kath Stam & Chris

Sunderlin, Midtown Utica Community Center; John Bartle, Luke Perry & David Chanatry, Utica College; Rev. Debbie Kelsey, Tabernacle Baptist Church; Shelley Callahan, The Center; Ryan Miller & Stacey Smith, thINCubator; and Erol Balkan & Paul Hagström, Hamilton College.

9 Tanvi Misra, *The Cities Refugees Saved*, BLOOMBERG CITYLAB (Jan. 31, 2019), www.bloomberg.com/news/articles/2019-01-31/resettled-refugees-grow-population-in-shrinking-cities.

10 Id.

11 La Corte, *supra* note 6 (citing Adele Peters, *Refugees Will Revitalize the Economy – If We Let Them*, FAST COMPANY (Mar. 15, 2016), www.fastcompany.com/3056324/refugees-will-revitalize-the-economy-if-we-let-them).

12 Misra, *supra* note 9.

13 *Immigrants and Refugees Revive Depressed Neighborhood*, VOA NEWS (Sept. 14, 2017), www.voanews.com/episode/immigrants-and-refugees-revive-depressed-neighborhood-3761101.

14 Melina Delkic, *"It's Not the Same": Why War Refugees Who Helped Revive St. Louis Are Leaving*, NEW YORK TIMES (Aug. 18, 2019), www.nytimes.com/2019/08/18/us/bosnian-refugees-st-louis-midwest.html.

15 Jacob McCleland, *How Vietnamese Refugees Spent 40 Years Rejuvenating an Oklahoma City Neighborhood*, KGOU (Dec. 30, 2015), www.kgou.org/oklahoma-news/2015-12-30/how-vietnamese-refugees-spent-40-years-rejuvenating-an-oklahoma-city-neighborhood#stream/0.

16 Katy Long, *This Small Town in America's Deep South Welcomes 1,500 Refugees a Year*, THE GUARDIAN (May 24, 2017), www.theguardian.com/us-news/2017/may/24/clarkston-georgia-refugee-resettlement-program.

17 *Afghan Refugees "Transform and Rejuvenate" Port Adelaide LGA*, UNIVERSITY OF SOUTH AUSTRALIA (Mar. 29, 2021),

www.unisa.edu.au/Media-Centre/Releases/2021/afghan-refugees-transform-and-rejuvenate-port-adelaide-lga.

18 *Afghanistan: Taliban "Tortured and Massacred" Men from Hazara Minority*, BBC NEWS (Aug. 20, 2021), www.bbc.com/news/world-asia-58277463.

19 Claudia Farhart, *Hazara Australians Fear Their People in Afghanistan Could Soon Be Massacred*, SBS NEWS (July 11, 2021), www.sbs.com.au/news/hazara-australians-fear-their-people-in-afghanistan-could-soon-be-massacred/b05ded74-5fe1-4ad7-b22a-617e94b41b56.

20 *Afghan Refugees "Transform and Rejuvenate" Port Adelaide LGA*, *supra* note 17 (quoting David Radford, lead author of the report).

21 Id. (quoting David Radford, lead author of the report).

22 Id.

23 Azrin Rahman, *11 Brilliant Startup Accelerators and Incubators for Migrant Entrepreneurs to Kick-Start*, STARTUPS WITHOUT BORDERS (Dec. 11, 2018), https://startupswb.com/blog/2018/12/11/11-brilliant-startup-accelerators-and-incubators-for-migrant-entrepreneurs.

24 Ahmad Sufian Bayram, ENTREPRENEURSHIP IN EXILE: INSIGHTS INTO SYRIAN REFUGEES' STARTUPS IN HOST COUNTRIES (2018).

25 Khadija Hamouchi, *Refugee Entrepreneurs Creating Financial Value across the World*, ARAB WEEKLY (June 13, 2019), https://thearabweekly.com/refugee-entrepreneurs-creating-financial-value-across-world.

26 Rahman, *supra* note 23 (citing Centre for Entrepreneurs, STARTING AFRESH: HOW ENTREPRENEURSHIP IS TRANSFORMING THE LIVES OF RESETTLED REFUGEES (2018)).

27 Julie Hirschfeld Davis & Somini Sengupta, *Trump Administration Rejects Study Showing Positive Impact of*

Refugees, NEW YORK TIMES (Sept. 18, 2017), www.nytimes
.com/2017/09/18/us/politics/refugees-revenue-cost-report-
trump.html (citing *Rejected Report Shows Revenue Brought In
by Refugees*, NEW YORK TIMES (Sept. 19, 2017), www.nytimes
.com/interactive/2017/09/19/us/politics/document-Refugee-
Report.html (draft of report by US Department of Health and
Human Services)).

28 Frank Mattern, Eckart Windhagen, Solveigh Hieronimus,
George Tsopelas, Jonathan Woetzel & Anu Madgavkar,
A Road Map for Integrating Europe's Refugees, MCKINSEY
GLOBAL INSTITUTE (Nov. 30, 2016), www.mckinsey.com/
featured-insights/employment-and-growth/a-road-map-for-
integrating-europes-refugees.

29 Bob Woods, *Despite Trump's Draconian Policies, Refugees
Continue Boosting New York's Rust Belt Economy*, CNBC (July 10,
2018), www.cnbc.com/2018/07/02/how-refugees-continue-
boosting-new-yorks-rust-belt-economy.html.

30 Id.

31 Centre for Entrepreneurs, STARTING AFRESH: HOW
ENTREPRENEURSHIP IS TRANSFORMING THE LIVES OF
RESETTLED REFUGEES (2018); *Faith Gakanje*, WORLD
ECONOMIC FORUM, www.wef.org.in/faith-gakanje; "*I Want to
See Women in the Lead*": *Faith Gakanje*, REFUGEE WEEK,
https://refugeeweek.org.uk/i-want-to-see-women-in-the-lead-
faith-gakanje.

32 Centre for Entrepreneurs, *supra* note 31.

33 *Refugee's Success as Producer of Middle Eastern Cheese*, AP
NEWS (May 1, 2017). Video provided at: www.youtube.com/
watch?v=b1gyQMUokHo.

34 *Syrian Refugees Launch New Social Enterprise in Toronto with
a Mission to Promote Refugee Employment and Help
Marginalized Communities*, PR NEWSWIRE (June 5, 2019),
www.prnewswire.com/news-releases/syrian-refugees-launch-

new-social-enterprise-in-toronto-with-a-mission-to-promote-refugee-employment-and-help-marginalized-communities-300862164.html.

35 Kara Bettis, *How Refugees Revived One White Iowa Church*, Christianity Today (July 29, 2016), www.christianitytoday.com/pastors/2016/july-web-exclusives/how-refugees-revived-one-white-iowa-church.html.

36 Id.

37 Author Interview with Rev. Debbie Kelsey, Tabernacle Baptist Church (Dec. 2018) (audio on file with author); *Utica Church Names Steeple to Honor Immigrants, Refugees*, Rome Sentinel (Apr. 28, 2018), https://romesentinel.com/stories/utica-church-names-steeple-to-honor-immigrants-refugees,6623.

38 Author Interview with Chris Sunderlin, Midtown Utica Community Center (Dec. 2018) (audio on file with author).

39 Farha Bhoyroo, *Afghan Doctor Helps Refugees Fight COVID-19, One Phone Call at a Time*, UNHCR (July 20, 2020), www.unhcr.org/news/stories/2020/7/5f155edc4/afghan-doctor-helps-refugees-fight-covid-19-phone-call-time.html.

40 Areez Tanbeen Rahman & Iffath Yeasmine, *Refugee Health Workers Lead COVID-19 Battle in Bangladesh Camps*, UNHCR (July 24, 2020), www.unhcr.org/news/stories/2020/7/5f198f1f4/refugee-health-workers-lead-covid-19-battle-bangladesh-camps.html.

41 Samuel Otieno Odhiambo, *Soap Maker in Kenya Refugee Camp Lowers Prices to Fight COVID-19*, UNHCR (May 20, 2020), www.unhcr.org/news/stories/2020/5/5ebe4f4a4/soap-maker-kenya-refugee-camp-lowers-prices-fight-covid-19.html.

42 Jessica Schulberg & Elise Foley, *How Houston's Refugees Are Facing Harvey – And Giving Back to the City That Took Them In*, Huffington Post (Aug. 30, 2017), www.huffpost.com/entry/harvey-texas-refugees_n_59a5d84be4b084581a141921.

43 Id.

44 Id.

45 New American Economy, Is There a Link Between Refugees and U.S. Crime Rates? (2017), https://research.newamericaneconomy.org/report/is-there-a-link-between-refugees-and-u-s-crime-rates.

46 Strochlic, *supra* note 2.

47 UNHCR, *Introduction to UNHCR Education Report 2016*, www.unhcr.org/en-us/introduction.html (citing UNESCO Institute for Statistics for global school enrollment rates).

48 Philip Bump, *64 Percent of Americans Want to Either Halt Syrian Refugees or Accept Only Christians*, Washington Post (Nov. 18, 2015), www.washingtonpost.com/news/the-fix/wp/2015/11/18/more-than-half-of-americans-want-to-halt-the-arrival-of-syrian-refugees.

49 Hebrews 13:2 (ESV).

Chapter 12 Dreams Become One

1 Warsan Shire, "Home." Poem provided at *Poem of the Day*, Medium (Sept. 11, 2017), https://medium.com/poem-of-the-day/warsan-shire-home-46630fcc90ab.

2 UNHCR, Zaatari Camp Fact Sheet (Sept. 2019), https://reliefweb.int/sites/reliefweb.int/files/resources/72077.pdf.

3 UNHCR, Za'atari Camp Fact Sheet (June 2021), https://reliefweb.int/report/jordan/unhcr-jordan-zaatari-refugee-camp-factsheet-june-2021; UNHCR, *Education at Za'atari Camp*, www.unhcr.org/7steps/en/education.

4 Id.

5 UNICEF, *Secondary Education* (Oct. 2019), https://data.unicef.org/topic/education/secondary-education.

6 *Education at Za'atari Camp*, *supra* note 3.

7 Tala Al-Rousan, Zaker Schwabkey, Lara Jirmanus & Brett D. Nelson, *Health Needs and Priorities of Syrian Refugees in Camps and Urban Settings in Jordan: Perspectives of Refugees and Health Care Providers*, 24 EASTERN MEDITERRANEAN HEALTH JOURNAL 243 (2018), https://pubmed.ncbi.nlm.nih.gov/29908019; UNHCR, *supra* note 3; *Health at Za'atari Camp*, UNHCR, www.unhcr.org/7steps/en/health.

8 UNHCR, ZAATARI CAMP FACT SHEET (Jan. 2017), https://reliefweb.int/sites/reliefweb.int/files/resources/FACTSHEET-ZaatariRefugeeCamp-January2017.pdf.

9 Al-Rousan, Schwabkey, Jirmanus & Nelson, *supra* note 7.

10 Australian Aid, REMOVING BARRIERS: THE PATH TOWARD INCLUSIVE ACCESS (2018).

11 *World's First Refugee Camp Playground for Disabled Kids*, AP NEWS (Nov. 4, 2018). Video provided at: www.youtube.com/watch?v=gKO2tuH1G6Q.

12 Claire McKeever, *UNICEF Opens First Inclusive Playground in Za'atari Refugee Camp*, UNICEF (Oct. 29, 2018), www.unicef.org/press-releases/unicef-opens-first-inclusive-playground-zaatari-refugee-camp-jordan.

13 *World's First Refugee Camp Playground for Disabled Kids*, *supra* note 11.

14 UNCHR, ADDRESSING CHILD MARRIAGE AND CHILD LABOR IN ZAATARI (2019).

15 Leymah Roberta Gbowee, *To Change the World, Let Refugee Women Lead*, PEACE WOMEN, www.peacewomen.org/resource/change-world-let-refugee-women-lead.

16 Asma, "We Dream of Peace."

Epilogue

1 Talea Miller, *Kiva Launches Multi-million Dollar World Refugee Fund on World Refugee Day*, KIVA, www.kiva.org/

blog/kiva-launches-multi-million-dollar-world-refugee-fund-on-world-refugee-day; *Refugees*, KIVA, www.refugees.kiva.org.

2 Refugee Investment Network, *What the RIN Does*, https://rin.wpengine.com/what-rin-does.

3 Social Performance Task Force, SERVING REFUGEE POPULATIONS IN LEBANON – LESSONS LEARNED FROM A NEW FRONTIER (2015), https://sptf.info/images/RefugeeWG-Al-Majmoua-case-study-final.pdf.

4 Oscar M. Sánchez Piñeiro, *How Business Incubators Can Facilitate Refugee Entrepreneurship and Integration*, UNHCR (Apr. 28, 2017), www.unhcr.org/innovation/how-we-can-use-business-incubators-for-refugee-integration.

5 Azrin Rahman, *11 Brilliant Startup Accelerators and Incubators for Migrant Entrepreneurs to Kick-Start*, STARTUPS WITHOUT BORDERS (Dec. 11, 2018), https://startupswb.com/blog/2018/12/11/11 brilliant-startup-accelerators-and-incubators-for-migrant-entrepreneurs.

6 Id.

7 Amplio Recruiting, https://ampliorecruiting.com.

8 Deborah Amos, *The Year the U.S. Refugee Resettlement Program Unraveled*, NPR (Jan. 1, 2018), npr.org/sections/parallels/2018/01/01/574658008/the-year-the-u-s-refugee-resettlement-program-unraveled.

INDEX

ABOUT THE AUTHOR

Painting by Malak

Andrew Leon Hanna is a first-generation Egyptian American lawyer, social entrepreneur, and author born and raised in Jacksonville, Florida. Hanna is cofounder and CEO of DreamxAmerica, joining storytelling and economic impact to highlight and support immigrant, refugee, and first-generation entrepreneurs. In this role, he cocreated and produced the *DreamxAmerica* documentary short film streaming on PBS, and created with Kiva US the DxA-Kiva Special Initiative to connect small businesses to zero-interest loans during the COVID-19 pandemic. Hanna previously founded the national education initiative IGNITE Peer Mentoring, was a consultant at McKinsey where he led the launch of the Generation global youth employment nonprofit in his hometown of Jacksonville, and was one of two US State Department delegates to represent the United States at the 7th UNESCO Youth Forum in Paris. Hanna has also served in the White House and US Justice Department.

Hanna is a Stanford Knight-Hennessy Scholar and Siebel Scholar at Stanford Graduate School of Business. He received a JD with honors from Harvard Law School, where he was an editor of the *Harvard Law Review*, and an AB with highest distinction in public policy from Duke University, where he was a Robertson Scholar and senior class president. Hanna has been named to the *Forbes* 30 Under 30 list, and was awarded the 2018 *Financial Times* and McKinsey Bracken Bower Prize for young authors at the National Gallery in London.